DICTION COACH

ARIAS FOR

MEZZO-SOPRANO

International Phonetic Alphabet and Diction Lessons
Recorded by a Professional, Native Speaker Coach

Diction Recordings
Corradina Caporello, Italian
Kathryn LaBouff, English
Irene Spiegelman, German
Pierre Vallet, French

International Phonetic Alphabet
Martha Gerhart, Italian and French
Kathryn LaBouff, English
Irene Spiegelman, German

This Diction Coach includes all arias from *Arias for Mezzo-Soprano* (HL50481098).
For plot notes and line-by-line translations, please see the original aria collection.

To access recorded diction lessons online, visit:
www.halleonard.com/mylibrary

Enter Code
5034-0416-6386-0234

ED 4404

On the cover: "L'opéra de Paris" by Raoul Dufy
Used by permission of The Phillips Collection, Washington D.C.

ISBN 978-1-4234-1309-7

www.schirmer.com
www.halleonard.com

G. SCHIRMER, *Inc.*

7777 W. BLUEMOUND RD. P.O. BOX 13819 MILWAUKEE, WI 53213

PREFACE

What a wonderful opportunity for singers these volumes represent. The diction coaches recorded are from the staffs of the Metropolitan Opera and The Juilliard School, whose specialty is working with singers. I personally have had the opportunity to study Italian with Ms. Caporello and have experienced the sheer delight of learning operatic texts with a
linguist who is devoted to the art of singing.

There are two versions of the text recorded for each aria.

1. Recitation

The Coach speaks the text of the aria as an actor would speak it, using spoken diction and capturing the mood. The guttural "R" is pronounced as in speech in French and German. Even in these free recitations, these experienced coaches are obviously informed as to how the text relates to the musical setting.

2. Diction Lessons

Dividing the text of the aria into short phrases, the coach speaks a line at a time very slowly and deliberately, without interpretation, making each word sound distinct. Time is allowed for the repetition of each phrase. In this slow version the French and German coaches adapt the guttural "R" in a manner appropriate for opera singers. The coaches in all languages make small adjustments recommended for singers in these slowly enunciated diction lessons, including elisions and liaisons between word sounds as related to the sung phrase.

There is not one universally used approach to International Phonetic Alphabet. The article before each language should be studied carefully for comprehension of the specific approach to IPA for each language in this edition.

The diction recordings can be used in many ways but a highly recommended plan is this. After carefully working regularly with the recorded diction lesson and the related IPA over several days, one should be able to reach fluency in the aria text. As an exercise separate from singing the aria, the singer should then speak the text freely, as in the diction coach's recitation. The singer likely will be inspired by the recitations recorded by the diction coaches, but after pronunciation is mastered might even begin to discover informed and individual interpretations in reciting the aria text.

By paying attention to the libretto of an aria, or an entire role, apart from the music, the opera singer can begin to understand character and interpretation in a way that would not be possible if the text is only considered by singing it. Just as an actor explores a script and a character from various historical, intellectual and emotional angles, so must the opera singer. Understanding the stated and unstated meanings of the text is fundamental in becoming a convincing actor on the opera stage, or on the opera audition stage. But the opera singer is only half done. After a thorough exploration of the words, one must discover how the composer interpreted the text and how best to express that interpretation. In great music for the opera stage, that exploration can be a fascinating lifetime journey.

Robert L. Larsen
June, 2008

CONTENTS

4 Audio Track List
6 About Italian IPA
26 About French IPA
45 About German IPA
50 About English IPA

ADRIANA LECOUVREUR
7 Acerba voluttà

THE BALLAD OF BABY DOE
52 Augusta! How can you turn away?

IL BARBIERE DI SIVIGLIA
8 Una voce poco fa

CARMEN
28 L'amour est un oiseau rebelle (Habanera)
30 Près des remparts de Séville (Seguidilla)
32 En vain, pour éviter

CAVALLERIA RUSTICANA
9 Voi lo sapete

LA CENERENTOLA
11 Non più mesta

THE CONSUL
54 Lullaby

COSÌ FAN TUTTE
12 Smanie implacabili

DIDO AND AENEAS
55 When I am laid in earth

FAUST
33 Faites-lui mes aveux

LA FAVORITA
13 O mio Fernando!

DIE FLEDERMAUS
48 Chacun à son goût

LA GIOCONDA
16 Voce di donna

LES HUGUENOTS
36 Nobles seigneurs, salut!

L'ITALIANA IN ALGERI
17 Cruda sorte!... Già so per pratica

LUCREZIA BORGIA
19 Il segreto per esser felici

THE MOTHER OF US ALL
56 We cannot retrace our steps

LE NOZZE DI FIGARO
20 Non so più cosa son
21 Voi, che sapete

ORFEO ED EURIDICE
22 Che farò senza Euridice?

ROMÉO ET JULIETTE
37 Que fais-tu, blanche tourterelle

THE SAINT OF BLEECKER STREET
58 Ah, Michele, don't you know

SAMSON ET DALILA
39 Printemps qui commence
41 Amour! viens aider ma faiblesse!
42 Mon cœur s'ouvre à ta voix

IL TROVATORE
24 Stride la vampa!

VANESSA
60 Must the winter come so soon?

WERTHER
44 Va! laisse couler mes larmes

ONLINE DICTION LESSONS

Audio Access Online includes a Recitation and a Diction Lesson for each aria.

Arias in Italian

ADRIANA LECOUVREUR
Acerba voluttà

IL BARBIERE DI SIVIGLIA
Una voce poco fa

CAVALLERIA RUSTICANA
Voi lo sapete

LA CENERENTOLA
Non più mesta

COSÌ FAN TUTTE
Smanie implacabili

LA FAVORITA
O mio Fernando!

LA GIOCONDA
Voce di donna

L'ITALIANA IN ALGERI
Cruda sorte!... Già so per pratica

LUCREZIA BORGIA
Il segreto per esser felici

LE NOZZE DI FIGARO
Non so più cosa son
Voi, che sapete

ORFEO ED EURIDICE
Che farò senza Euridice?

IL TROVATORE
Stride la vampa!

Arias in French

CARMEN
L'amour est un oiseau rebelle (Habanera)
Près des remparts de Séville (Seguidilla)

ONLINE DICTION LESSONS

Arias in French (cont.)

CARMEN
En vain, pour éviter

FAUST
Faites-lui mes aveux

LES HUGUENOTS
Nobles seigneurs, salut!

ROMÉO ET JULIETTE
Que fais-tu, blanche tourterelle

SAMSON ET DALILA
Printemps qui commence
Amour! viens aider ma faiblesse!
Mon cœur s'ouvre à ta voix

WERTHER
Va! laisse couler mes larmes

Aria in German

DIE FLEDERMAUS
Chacun à son goût

Arias in English

THE BALLAD OF BABY DOE
Augusta! How can you turn away?

THE CONSUL
Lullaby

DIDO AND AENEAS
When I am laid in earth

THE MOTHER OF US ALL
We cannot retrace our steps

THE SAINT OF BLEECKER STREET
Ah, Michele, don't you know

VANESSA
Must the winter come so soon?

ABOUT THE ITALIAN IPA TRANSLITERATIONS

by Martha Gerhart

While the IPA is currently the diction learning tool of choice for singers not familiar with the foreign languages in which they sing, differences in transliterations exist in diction manuals and on the internet, just as differences of pronunciation exist in the Italian language itself.

The Italian transliterations in this volume reflect the following choices:

All unstressed "e's" and "o's" are *closed*. This choice is based on the highest form of the spoken language, as in the authoritative Italian dictionary edited by Zingarelli. However, in practice, singers may well make individual choices as to *closed* or *open* depending upon the vocal tessitura and technical priorities.

Also, there are many Italian words (such as "sento," "cielo," and etc.) for which, in practice, both *closed* and *open* vowels in the *stressed* syllable are perfectly acceptable.

The "nasal 'm'" symbol [ɱ], indicating that the letter "n" assimilates before a "v" or an "f" (such as "inferno" becoming [im ˈfɛr no] in execution, is not used in these transliterations. This choice was a practical one to avoid confusion on the part of the student who might wonder why "in" is transcribed as if it were "im," unlike in any dictionary. However, students are encouraged to use the [ɱ] as advised by experts.

Double consonants which result, in execution, from *phrasal doubling* (*raddoppiamento sintattico*) are not transliterated as such; but students should utilize this sophistication of Italian lyric diction as appropriate.

The syllabic divisions in these transliterations are in the interest of encouraging the singer to lengthen the vowel before a single consonant rather than making an incorrect double consonant, and also to encourage the singer, when there are two consonants, the first of which is *l, m, n*, or *r*, to give more strength to the first of those two consonants.

Intervocalic "s's" are transliterated as *voiced*, despite the fact that in many words ("casa," "così," etc.) the "s" is *unvoiced* in the language (and in the above-mentioned dictionary). Preferred practice for singers is to *voice* those "s's" in the interest of legato; yet, an unvoiced "s" pronunciation in those cases is not incorrect. (*Note*: words which combine a prefix and a stem beginning with an unvoiced "s" ["risolvi," "risanare," etc.] retain the unvoiced "s" of the prefix in singing as well as in speech.)

Many Italian words have alternate pronunciations given in the best dictionaries, particularly regarding closed or open vowels. In my IPA transliterations I chose the first given pronunciation, which is not always the preferred pronunciation in common Italian usage as spoken by Corradina Caporello on the accompanying CDs. I defer to my respected colleague in all cases for her expert pronunciation of beautiful Italian diction.

Pronunciation Key

IPA Symbol	Approximate sound in English	IPA Symbol	Approximate sound in English
[i]	feet	[s]	set
[e]	potato	[z]	zip
[ɛ]	bed	[l]	lip
[a]	father	[ʎ]	million
[ɔ]	taut		
[o]	tote	[ɾ]	as *British* "very" – flipped "r"
[u]	tube	[r]	no English equivalent – rolled "r"
[j]	Yale		
[w]	watch	[n]	name
		[m]	mop
[b]	beg	[ŋ]	anchor
[p]	pet	[ɲ]	onion
[d]	deep	[tʃ]	cheese
[t]	top	[dʒ]	George
[g]	Gordon	[dz]	feeds
[k]	kit	[ts]	fits
[v]	vet		
[f]	fit	[ː]	indicates doubled consonants
[ʃ]	she	[ˈ]	indicates the primary stress; the syllable following the mark is stressed

ADRIANA LECOUVREUR

music: Francesco Cilea
libretto: Arturo Colautti (after the play by Eugène Scribe and Gabriel Jean Baptiste Legouvé)

Acerba voluttà

a ˈtʃɛr ba	vo lut: ˈta	ˈdol tʃe	tor ˈtu ɾa
Acerba	**voluttà,**	**dolce**	**tortura,**
harsh	*pleasure*	*sweet*	*torment*

len ˈtis: si ma	a go ˈni a	ra ˈpi da	of: ˈfe za
lentissima	**agonia,**	**rapida**	**offesa,**
drawn out	*agony*	*quick*	*violation*

ˈvam pa	ˈdʒɛ lo	tre ˈmor	ˈzma nja	pa ˈu ɾa
vampa,	**gelo,**	**tremor,**	**smania,**	**paura,**
fire	*ice*	*agitation*	*frenzy*	*fear*

a da mo ˈɾo zo	sen	ˈtor na	lat: ˈte za
ad amoroso	**sen**	**torna**	**l'attesa!**
to the loving	*breast*	*brings back*	*the wait*

ˈoɲ: ɲi	ˈɛ ko	ˈoɲ: ɲi	ˈom bra	ˈnel: la	ˈnɔt: te	in ˈtʃe za
Ogni	**eco,**	**ogni**	**ombra**	**nella**	**notte**	**incesa**
every	*echo*	*every*	*shadow*	*in the*	*night*	*burning*

ˈkon tro	la	im pat: ˈtsjɛn te	ˈal ma	kon ˈdʒu ɾa
contro	**la**	**impaziente**	**alma**	**congiura:**
against	*the*	*impatient*	*soul*	*conspires*

fra	dub: ˈbjet: tsa	e	de ˈzi o	ˈtut: ta	so ˈspe za
fra	**dubbiezza**	**e**	**desìo**	**tutta**	**sospesa,**
between	*doubt*	*and*	*desire*	*everything*	*suspended*

le ter ni ˈta	nel: ˈlat: ti mo	mi ˈzu ɾa
l'eternità	**nell'attimo**	**misura.**
the eternity	*in the moment*	*it measures*

ver: ra	mo ˈbli a
Verrà?	**M'oblia?**
he will come	*me he forgets*

saf: ˈfret: ta
S'affretta?
he hurries

o	pur	si ˈpɛn te
O	**pur**	**si pente?**
or	*perhaps*	*he changes his mind*

ˈɛk: ko	ˈeʎ: ʎi	ˈdʒun dʒe
Ecco,	**egli**	**giunge!**
look	*he*	*arrives*

nɔ	del	ˈfju me	ɛ	il	ˈvɛr so
No,	**del**	**fiume**	**è**	**il**	**verso,**
no	*of the*	*river*	*it is*	*the*	*sound*

ˈmi sto	al	so ˈspir	dun	ar ˈbo ɾe	dor ˈmɛn te
misto	**al**	**sospir**	**d'un**	**arbore**	**dormente.**
mixed	*with the*	*sigh*	*of a*	*tree*	*sleeping*

o	va ga ˈbon da	ˈstel: la	do ˈɾjɛn te
O	**vagabonda**	**stella**	**d'Oriente,**
o	*vagrant*	*star*	*of East*

non tra mon ˈtar
non tramontar;
not to wane

sor: ˈri di al: lu ni ˈvɛr so
sorridi all'universo,
smile at the universe

e ˈseʎ: ʎi non ˈmɛn te
e s'egli non mente,
and if he not lies

ˈskor ta il ˈmi o a ˈmor
scorta il mio amor!
escort the my love

IL BARBIERE DI SIVIGLIA

music: Gioachino Rossini
libretto: Cesare Sterbini (after *Le Barbier de Séville*, a comedy by Pierre Augustin Caron de Beaumarchais)

Una voce poco fa

ˈu na ˈvo tʃe ˈpɔ ko fa
Una voce poco fa
a voice a little while ago

kwi nel kɔr mi ri swo ˈnɔ
qui nel cor mi risuonò;
here in the heart to me resounded

il ˈmi o kɔr fe ˈɾi to ɛ dʒa
il mio cor ferito è già,
the my heart wounded is now

e lin ˈdɔr fu ke il pja ˈgɔ
e Lindor fu che il piagò.
and Lindor was who it covered with wounds

si lin ˈdɔ ɾo ˈmi o sa ˈɾa
Sì, Lindoro mio sarà,
yes Lindoro mine will be

lo dʒu ˈɾa i la vin tʃe ˈɾɔ
lo giurai, la vincerò.
it I swore it I shall win

il tu ˈtor ri ku ze ˈɾa
Il tutor ricuserà,
the guardian will refuse

ˈi o lin ˈdʒeɲ: ɲo a gut: tse ˈɾɔ
io l'ingegno aguzzerò;
I the wit [I] will sharpen

ˈal: la fin sak: ke te ˈɾa
alla fin s'accheterà,
in the end he will calm down

e kon ˈten ta ˈi o re ste ˈɾɔ
e contenta io resterò.
and content I [I] will remain

ˈi o	ˈso no	ˈdɔ tʃi le
Io	**sono**	**docile,**
I	*[I] am*	*docile*

son	ri spetː ˈto za
son	**rispettosa,**
I am	*respectful*

ˈso no	ubː bi ˈdjɛn te
sono	**ubbidiente,**
I am	*obedient*

ˈdol tʃe	a mo ˈɾo za
dolce,	**amorosa;**
sweet	*affectionate*

mi	ˈlaʃː ʃo	ˈrɛdː dʒe ɾe
mi	**lascio**	**reggere,**
me	*I allow*	*to govern*

mi	fɔ	gwi ˈdar
mi	**fo**	**guidar.**
me	*I make*	*to guide*

ma	se	mi	ˈtokː ka no
Ma	**se**	**mi**	**toccano**
but	*if*	*me*	*they touch*

do ˈvɛ	il	ˈmi o	ˈde bo le
dove'è	**il**	**mio**	**debole,**
where is	*the*	*my*	*weakness*

sa ˈɾɔ	ˈu na	ˈvi pe ɾa
sarò	**una**	**vipera,**
I will be	*a*	*viper*

e	ˈtʃɛn to	ˈtrapː po le
e	**cento**	**trappole**
and	*hundred*	*tricks*

ˈpri ma	di	ˈtʃɛ de ɾe	fa ˈɾɔ	dʒo ˈkar
prima	**di**	**cedere**	**farò**	**giocar.**
before	*of*	*to yield*	*I will make*	*to play*

CAVALLERIA RUSTICANA

music: Pietro Mascagni
libretto: Giovanni Targioni-Tozzetti and Guido Menasci (after a story by Giovanni Verga)

Voi lo sapete

ˈvo i	lo	sa ˈpe te	o	ˈmamː ma
Voi	**lo**	**sapete,**	**o**	**mamma:**
you	*it*	*[you] know*	*oh*	*mamma*

ˈpri ma	dan ˈdar	sol ˈda to
prima	**d'andar**	**soldato**
before	*of to go*	*soldier*

tu ˈɾidː du	a ˈve va	a	ˈlɔ la
Turiddu	**aveva**	**a**	**Lola**
Turiddu	*had*	*to*	*Lola*

e ˈtɛr na fe dʒu ˈɾa to
eterna fè giurato.
eternal faith sworn

tor ˈnɔ la ˈsɛpː pe ˈspɔ za
Tornò, la seppe sposa;
he returned her he learned wife

e kon un ˈnwɔ vo a ˈmo ɾe
e con un nuovo amore
and with a new love

ˈvɔlː le ˈspeɲː ɲer la ˈfjamː ma
volle spegner la fiamma
he wanted to extinguish the flame

ke ʎi bru ˈtʃa va il ˈkɔ ɾe
che gli bruciava il core.
that to him was burning the heart

ma ˈmɔ la ˈma i a
M'amò. L'amai. Ah!
me he loved him I loved ah

kwelː ˈlin vi da
Quell'invida
that woman envious

ˈdoɲː ɲi de ˈlitː tsja ˈmi a
d'ogni delizia mia,
of every delight mine

del ˈsu o ˈspɔ zo di ˈmen ti ka
del suo sposo dimentica.
of the her husband she forgets

ˈar se di dʒe lo ˈzi a
Arse di gelosia;
she burned with jealousy

me la ra ˈpi to
me l'ha rapito!
from me him she has stolen

ˈpri va delː lo ˈnor ˈmi o ri ˈmaŋ go
Priva dell'onor mio rimango.
deprived of the honor mine I remain

ˈlɔ la e tu ˈɾidː du ˈsa ma no
Lola e Turiddu s'amano;
Lola and Turiddu each other they love

ˈi o ˈpjaŋ go
io piango.
I [I] weep

ˈi o son danː ˈna ta
Io son dannata.
I [I] am damned

LA CENERENTOLA

music: Gioachino Rossini
libretto: Jacopo Ferretti (after Charles Guillaume Etienne's libretto for *Cendrillon* by Nicolas Isouard, also after the fairy tale)

Non più mesta

ˈna kwi	alː lafː ˈfanː no	e	al	ˈpjan to
Nacqui	**all'affanno**	**e**	**al**	**pianto.**
I was born	*to the suffering*	*and*	*to the*	*weeping*

sofː ˈfri	ta ˈtʃɛn do	il	ˈkɔ ɾe
Soffrì	**tacendo**	**il**	**core;**
[it] suffered	*being silent*	*the*	*heart*

ma	per	so ˈa ve	iŋ ˈkan to
ma	**per**	**soave**	**incanto**
but	*through*	*sweet*	*magic*

delː le ˈta	ˈmi a	nel	ˈfjo ɾe
dell'età	**mia**	**nel**	**fiore,**
of the age	*mine*	*in the*	*flower*

ˈko me	un	ba ˈle no	ˈra pi do
come	**un**	**baleno**	**rapido**
like	*a*	*lightning*	*rapid*

la	ˈsɔr te	ˈmi a	kan ˈdʒɔ
la	**sorte**	**mia**	**cangiò.**
the	*destiny*	*mine*	*changed*

nɔ	nɔ	nɔ	nɔ
No,	**no,**	**no,**	**no:**
no	*no*	*no*	*no*

ter ˈdʒe te	il	ˈtʃiʎː ʎo
tergete	**il**	**ciglio;**
wipe dry	*the*	*eye*

per ˈke	tre ˈmar
perchè	**tremar?**
why	*to tremble*

a	ˈkwe sto	sen	vo ˈla te
A	**questo**	**sen**	**volate;**
to	*this*	*breast*	*fly*

ˈfiʎː ʎa	so ˈɾɛlː la	a ˈmi ka
figlia,	**sorella,**	**amica—**
daughter	*sister*	*friend*

ˈtutː to	tro ˈva te	in	me
tutto	**trovate**	**in**	**me.**
all	*you find*	*in*	*me*

non	pju	ˈmɛ sta	akː ˈkan to al	ˈfwɔ ko
Non	**più**	**mesta**	**accanto al**	**fuoco**
not	*more*	*sad*	*beside [at] the*	*fire*

sta ˈɾɔ	ˈso la	a	gor gedː ˈdʒar	nɔ
starò	**sola**	**a**	**gorgheggiar,**	**no.**
I will be	*alone*	*to*	*[to] warble*	*no*

a	fu	un	ˈlam po	un	ˈsoɲ: ɲo	un	ˈdʒwɔ ko
Ah	**fu**	**un**	**lampo,**	**un**	**sogno,**	**un**	**giuoco**
ah	*was*	*a*	*flash*	*a*	*dream*	*a*	*game*

il	ˈmi o	ˈluŋ go	pal pi ˈtar
il	**mio**	**lungo**	**palpitar.**
the	*my*	*long*	*trepidation*

COSÌ FAN TUTTE

music: Wolfgang Amadeus Mozart
libretto: Lorenzo da Ponte

Smanie implacabili

a	ˈskɔ sta ti
Ah,	**scostati!**
ah	*move [yourself] away*

pa ˈvɛn ta	il	ˈtri sto	ef: ˈfɛt: to
Paventa	**il**	**tristo**	**effetto**
fear	*the*	*sad*	*effect*

dun	di spe ˈɾa to	af: ˈfɛt: to
d'un	**disperato**	**affetto!**
of a	*desperate*	*affection*

ˈkju di	ˈkwel: le	fi ˈnɛ stre
Chiudi	**quelle**	**finestre—**
close	*those*	*windows*

ˈɔ djo	la	ˈlu tʃe
odio	**la**	**luce,**
I hate	*the*	*light*

ˈɔ djo	ˈla ɾja	ke	ˈspi ɾo
odio	**l'aria**	**che**	**spiro—**
I hate	*the air*	*that*	*I breathe*

ˈɔ djo	me	ˈstes: sa
odio	**me**	**stessa!**
I hate	*me*	*myself*

ki	sker ˈniʃ: ʃe	il	ˈmi o	dwɔl
Chi	**schernisce**	**il**	**mio**	**duol,**
who	*mocks*	*the*	*my*	*grief*

ki	mi	kon ˈso la
chi	**mi**	**consola?**
who	*me*	*consoles*

dɛ	ˈfud: dʒi	per	pje ˈta
Deh	**fuggi,**	**per**	**pietà;**
ah	*flee*	*for*	*pity's sake*

ˈlaʃ: ʃa mi	ˈso la
lasciami	**sola.**
leave me	*alone*

ˈzman je	im pla ˈka bi li
Smanie	**implacabili**
frenzies	*implacable*

ke	ma dʒi ˈta te
che	**m'agitate,**
which	*me agitate*

ˈen tro	kwe ˈsta ni ma
entro	**quest'anima**
within	*this soul*

pju	non	tʃes: ˈsa te
più	**non**	**cessate**
more	*not*	*cease*

fiŋ ˈke	laŋ ˈgɔʃ: ʃa
finchè	**l'angoscia**
until	*the anguish*

mi	fa	mo ˈɾir
mi	**fa**	**morir.**
me	*makes*	*to die*

e ˈzɛm pjo	ˈmi ze ɾo
Esempio	**misero**
example	*miserable*

da ˈmor	fu ˈnɛ sto
d'amor	**funesto**
of love	*funereal*

da ˈɾɔ	al: le u ˈmɛ ni di
darò	**all'Eumenidi**
I shall give	*to the Eumenides*

se	ˈvi va	ˈrɛ sto
se	**viva**	**resto**
if	*alive*	*I remain*

kol	ˈswɔ no	or: ˈri bi le
col	**suono**	**orribile**
with	*sound*	*horrible*

de	ˈmjɛ i	so ˈspir
de'	**miei**	**sospir.**
of [the]	*my*	*sighs*

LA FAVORITA

music: Gaetano Donizetti
libretto: Alphonse Royer, Gustave Vaëz, and Eugène Scribe (after Baculard d'Arnaud's play *La Comte de Comminges,* and partly based on Eugène Scribe's libretto for *L'Ange de Nisida* by Donizetti)

O mio Fernando!

ˈfi a	ˈduŋ kwe	ˈve ɾo	o	tʃɛl
Fia	**dunque**	**vero,**	**oh**	**ciel?**
be it	*then*	*true*	*o*	*heaven*

ˈdes: so	fer ˈnan do	lo	ˈspɔ zo	di	le o ˈnɔ ɾa
Desso,	**Fernando,**	**lo**	**sposo**	**di**	**Leonora!**
this one	*Fernando*	*the*	*husband*	*of*	*Leonora*

a	ˈtut: to	mel	ˈdi tʃe
Ah!	**Tutto**	**mel**	**dice,**
ah	*everything*	*to me it*	*says*

e ˈdubː bja ɛ ˈlal ma aŋ ˈko ɾa
e dubbia è l'alma ancora
and uncertain is the soul still

alː li natː ˈte za ˈdʒɔ ja
all'inattesa gioia!
at the unexpected joy

o ˈdi o spo ˈzar lo
Oh Dio! Sposarlo?
oh God to marry him

o ˈmi a ver ˈgoɲː ɲa e ˈstrɛ ma
Oh mia vergogna estrema!
oh my shame extreme

in ˈdɔ te al ˈprɔ de re ˈkar il di zo ˈnor
In dote al prode recar il disonor—
in dowry to the valiant one to bring the dishonor

nɔ ˈma i
no, mai;
no never

do ˈvesː se e ze ˈkrar mi fudː ˈdʒir
dovesse esecrarmi, fuggir,
should he to abhor me to flee

sa ˈpra in brɛ ˈvo ɾa
saprà in brev'ora
he will know in brief hour

ki ˈsi a la ˈdɔnː na
chi sia la donna
who be the woman

ke ko ˈtan to a ˈdo ɾa
che cotanto adora.
whom so much [he] adores

o ˈmi o fer ˈnan do
O mio Fernando!
oh my Fernando

ˈdelː la ˈtɛrː ra il ˈtrɔ no a posː se ˈder ti
Della terra il trono a possederti
of the country the throne to [to] possess with you

a ˈvri a do ˈna to il kɔr
avria donato il cor;
I would have given the heart

ma ˈpu ɾo la ˈmor ˈmi o ˈko me il per ˈdo no
ma puro l'amor mio come il perdono,
but pure the love mine like the pardon

danː ˈna to ˈa i ˈlasː sa ɛ a
dannato, ahi lassa! è a
damned miserable me is to

di spe ˈɾa to orː ˈror
disperato orror.
desperate horror

il ver ˈfi a ˈnɔ to
Il ver fia noto,
the truth may [it] be noted

e in ˈtu o di ˈsprɛ dʒo e ˈstrɛ mo
e in tuo dispregio estremo,
and in your contempt extreme

la ˈpe na a ˈvrɔm: mi
la pena avrommi
the pain I shall have to me

ke mad: ˈdʒor si de a
che maggior si de', ah!
which most itself must [be] ah

se il ˈdʒu sto ˈtu o diz ˈdeɲ:ɲo
Se il giusto tuo disdegno
if the justified your disdain

al: ˈlor ˈfi a ˈʃe mo
allor fia scemo,
still be lacking

ˈpjom bi gran ˈdi o
piombi, gran Dio,
let fall great God

la ˈfol gor ˈtu a su me
la folgor tua su me!
the thunderbolt yours on me

su kru ˈdɛ li e ki var: ˈrɛ sta
Su, crudeli, e chi v'arresta?
come on cruel ones and who you stops

ˈskrit: to ɛ in ˈtʃɛ lo il ˈmi o do ˈlor
Scritto è in cielo il mio dolor!
written is in heaven the my grief

su ve ˈni te el: ˈlɛ ˈu na ˈfɛ sta
Su, venite, ell'è una festa;
come on come it is a celebration

ˈspar sa ˈla ɾa ˈsi a di fjor
sparsa l'ara sia di fior.
strewn the altar may be with flowers

dʒa la ˈtom ba a me sap: ˈprɛ sta
Già la tomba a me s'appresta;
already the tomb for me itself readies

ri ko ˈpɛr ta in ˈne gro vel ˈsia
ricoperta in negro vel sia
covered in black veil may be

la ˈtri sta fi dan ˈtsa ta ke re ˈjɛt: ta
la trista fidanzata che reietta,
the sad betrothed one who rejected

di spe ˈɾa ta non a ˈvra per ˈdo no in tʃɛl
disperata, non avrà perdono in ciel.
despairing not will have pardon in heaven

ma le ˈdetː ta	di spe ˈɾa ta
Maledetta,	**disperata,**
cursed	*despairing*

non	a ˈvra	per ˈdo no	in	tʃɛl
non	**avrà**	**perdono**	**in**	**ciel.**
not	*[she] will have*	*pardon*	*in*	*heaven*

a	kru ˈdɛ li	e	ki	varː ˈrɛ sta
Ah!	**crudeli,**	**e**	**chi**	**v'arresta?**
ah	*cruel ones*	*and*	*who*	*you stops*

ˈskritː to	in	ˈtʃɛ lo	ɛ	il	ˈmi o	do ˈlor
Scritto	**in**	**cielo**	**è**	**il**	**mio**	**dolor.**
written	*in*	*heaven*	*is*	*the*	*my*	*grief*

kru ˈdɛ li	ve ˈni te
Crudeli,	**venite.**
cruel ones	*come*

a	la	ˈtri sta	fi dan ˈtsa ta
Ah!	**la**	**trista**	**fidanzata**
ah	*the*	*sad*	*betrothed one*

non	a ˈvra	per ˈdo no	in	tʃɛl
non	**avrà**	**perdono**	**in**	**ciel.**
not	*will have*	*pardon*	*in*	*heaven*

LA GIOCONDA

music: Amilcare Ponchielli
libretto: "Tobia Gorria," a pseudonym for Arrigo Boito (after *Angelo, Tyran de Padoue* by Victor Hugo)

Voce di donna

ˈvo tʃe	di	ˈdɔnː na	o	ˈdan dʒe lo
Voce	**di**	**donna**	**o**	**d'angelo**
voice	*of*	*woman*	*or*	*of angel*

le	ˈmi e	ka ˈte ne	a	ˈʃɔl to
le	**mie**	**catene**	**ha**	**sciolto;**
the	*my*	*fetters*	*has*	*loosened*

mi	ˈvjɛ tan	le	ˈmi e	ˈtɛ ne bre
mi	**vietan**	**le**	**mie**	**tenebre**
to me	*prohibit*	*the*	*my*	*darknesses*

di	ˈkwelː la	ˈsan ta	il	ˈvol to
di	**quella**	**santa**	**il**	**volto,**
of	*that*	*saintly one*	*the*	*face*

ˈpu ɾe	da	me	non	ˈpar ta si
pure	**da**	**me**	**non**	**partasi**
yet	*from*	*me*	*not*	*may she part*

ˈsɛn tsa	un	pje ˈto zo	don	nɔ
senza	**un**	**pietoso**	**don,**	**no!**
without	*a*	*compassionate*	*gift*	*no*

a	te	ˈkwe sto	ro ˈza ɾjo
A	**te**	**questo**	**rosario**
to	*you*	*this*	*rosary*

ke	le	pre ˈɡjɛ ɾe	a ˈdu na
che	**le**	**preghiere**	**aduna.**
which	*the*	*prayers*	*brings together*

ˈi o	te	lo	ˈpɔr go
Io	**te**	**lo**	**porgo—**
I	*to you*	*it*	*[I] offer*

at: ˈtʃɛt: ta lo
accettalo;
accept it

ti	por te ˈɾa	for ˈtu na
ti	**porterà**	**fortuna.**
to you	*it will bring*	*[good] fortune*

ˈsul: la	ˈtu a	ˈtɛ sta	ˈvi dʒi li
Sulla	**tua**	**testa**	**vigili**
over the	*your*	*head*	*may keep watch*

la	ˈmi a	be ne dit: ˈtsjon
la	**mia**	**benedizion.**
the	*my*	*blessing*

L’ITALIANA IN ALGERI

music: Gioachino Rossini
libretto: Angeli Anelli (originally for Luigi Mosca’s 1808 opera of the same name)

Cruda sorte!... Già so per pratica

ˈkru da	ˈsɔr te	a ˈmor	ti ˈɾan: no
Cruda	**sorte!**	**Amor**	**tiranno!**
harsh	*fate*	*love*	*tyrannical*

ˈkwe sto	ɛ	il	ˈprɛ mjo	di	ˈmi a	fe
Questo	**è**	**il**	**premio**	**di**	**mia**	**fe’:**
this	*is*	*the*	*prize*	*of*	*my*	*fidelity*

non	vɛ	or: ˈror	ter: ˈror
non	**v’è**	**orror,**	**terror,**
not	*there is*	*horror*	*terror*

ne	af: ˈfan: no
nè	**affanno**
nor	*anguish*

ˈpa ɾi	a	kwel	ˈki o	ˈprɔ vo	in	me
pari	**a**	**quel**	**ch’io**	**provo**	**in**	**me.**
equal	*to*	*that*	*which I*	*[I] feel*	*in*	*me*

per	te	ˈso lo	o	ˈmi o	lin ˈdɔ ɾo
Per	**te**	**solo,**	**o**	**mio**	**Lindoro,**
for	*you*	*alone*	*o*	*my*	*Lindoro*

ˈi o	mi	ˈtrɔ vo	in	tal	pe ˈɾiʎ: ʎo
io	**mi**	**trovo**	**in**	**tal**	**periglio;**
I	*myself*	*[I] find*	*in*	*such*	*peril*

da	ki	ˈspɛ ɾo	o	ˈdi o	kon ˈsiʎ: ʎo
da	**chi**	**spero,**	**oh**	**Dio!**	**consiglio?**
from	*whom*	*I hope*	*oh*	*God*	*advice*

ki	kon ˈfɔr to	mi	da ˈɾa
Chi	**conforto**	**mi**	**darà?**
who	*comfort*	*to me*	*will give*

kwa	tʃi vwɔl	di zin vol ˈtu ɾa
Qua	**ci vuol**	**disinvoltura;**
here	*is needed*	*agility*

non	pju	ˈzman je	ne	pa ˈu ɾa
non	**più**	**smanie,**	**nè**	**paura:**
not	*more*	*frenzies*	*nor*	*fear*

di	ko ˈɾad: dʒo	ɛ	ˈtɛm po	a ˈdɛs: so
di	**coraggio**	**è**	**tempo**	**adesso...**
of	*courage*	*it is*	*time*	*now*

or	ki	ˈso no	si ve ˈdra
or	**chi**	**sono**	**si vedrà.**
now	*who*	*I am*	*one shall see*

dʒa	sɔ	per	ˈpra ti ka
Già	**so**	**per**	**pratica**
already	*I know*	*through*	*experience*

kwal	ˈsi a	lef: ˈfɛt: to
qual	**sia**	**l'effetto**
what	*be*	*the effect*

dun	ˈzgwar do	ˈlaŋ gwi do
d'un	**sguardo**	**languido,**
of a	*glance*	*languid*

dun	so spi ˈɾet: to
d'un	**sospiretto.**
of a	*little sigh*

sɔ	a	do ˈmar	ʎi	ˈwɔ mi ni	ˈko me	si fa
So	**a**	**domar**	**gli**	**uomini**	**come**	**si fa,**
I know	*to*	*[to] tame*	*the*	*men*	*how*	*[it] is done*

si	sɔ	a	do ˈmar	ʎi	ˈwɔ mi ni	ˈko me	si fa
sì,	**so**	**a**	**domar**	**gli**	**uomini**	**come**	**si fa.**
yes	*I know*	*to*	*[to] tame*	*the*	*men*	*how*	*[it] is done*

ˈsi en	ˈdol tʃi	o	ˈru vi di
Sien	**dolci**	**o**	**ruvidi,**
be they	*gentle*	*or*	*rough*

ˈsi en	ˈflɛm: ma	o	ˈfɔ ko
sien	**flemma**	**o**	**foco,**
be they	*coolness*	*or*	*fire*

son	ˈtut: ti	ˈsi mi li	a ˈprɛs: so a ˈpɔ ko
son	**tutti**	**simili**	**a presso a poco.**
they are	*all*	*alike*	*approximately*

ˈtut: ti	la	ˈkjɛ do no
Tutti	**la**	**chiedono,**
all	*it*	*they ask for*

ˈtut: ti	la	ˈbra ma no
tutti	**la**	**bramano**
all	*it*	*they desire*

da	ˈva ga	ˈfem: mi na	fe li tʃi ˈta
da	**vaga**	**femmina**	**felicità.**
from	*lovely*	*woman*	*happiness*

si	si
Sì	**sì...**
yes	*yes*

LUCREZIA BORGIA

music: Gaetano Donizetti
libretto: Felice Romani (after the tragedy *Lucrèce Borgia* by Victor Hugo)

Il segreto per esser felici
(Brindisi)

il	se ˈgre to	per	ˈɛs: ser	fe ˈli tʃi
Il	**segreto**	**per**	**esser**	**felici**
the	*secret*	*for*	*to be*	*happy*

sɔ	per	ˈprɔ va
so	**per**	**prova**
I know	*through*	*practice*

e	lin ˈseɲ: ɲo	ˈaʎ: ʎi	a ˈmi tʃi
e	**l'insegno**	**agli**	**amici.**
and	*it I teach*	*to the*	*friends*

ˈsi a	se ˈɾe no	ˈsi a	ˈnu bi lo	il	ˈtʃɛ lo
Sia	**sereno,**	**sia**	**nubilo**	**il**	**cielo,**
be it	*clear*	*be it*	*cloudy*	*the*	*sky*

ˈoɲ: ɲi	ˈtɛm po	ˈsi a	ˈkal do	ˈsi a	ˈdʒɛ lo
ogni	**tempo,**	**sia**	**caldo,**	**sia**	**gelo,**
every	*weather*	*be it*	*hot*	*be it*	*icy*

ˈsker tso	e	ˈbe vo
scherzo	**e**	**bevo,**
I joke	*and*	*I drink*

e	de ˈɾi do	ʎin ˈsa ni
e	**derido**	**gl'insani**
and	*I mock*	*the crazy ones*

ke	si	dan	del	fu ˈtu ɾo
che	**si**	**dan**	**del**	**futuro**
who	*themselves*	*devote [to]*	*of the*	*future*

pen ˈsjɛr
pensier.
thought

non	ku ˈɾja mo	lin ˈtʃɛr to	do ˈma ni
Non	**curiamo**	**l'incerto**	**domani,**
not	*let us care about*	*the uncertain*	*tomorrow*

se	kwe ˈstɔd: dʒi	nɛ	ˈda to	go ˈder
se	**quest'oggi**	**n'è**	**dato**	**goder.**
if	*this today*	*of it it is*	*given*	*to enjoy*

pro fit: ˈtja mo	deʎ: ˈʎan: ni	fjo ˈɾɛn ti
Profittiamo	**degl'anni**	**fiorenti;**
let us profit	*from the years*	*flowering*

il	pja ˈtʃer	li	fa	ˈkor: rer	pju	ˈlɛn ti
il	**piacer**	**li**	**fa**	**correr**	**più**	**lenti.**
the	*pleasure*	*them*	*makes*	*to pass by*	*more*	*slow*

se	vek: ˈkjet: tsa	kon	ˈli vi da	ˈfat: tʃa
Se	**vecchiezza**	**con**	**livida**	**faccia**
if	*old age*	*with*	*sullen*	*face*

ˈstam: mi	a ˈtɛr go
stammi	**a tergo**
stands to me	*behind*

e	ˈmi a	ˈvi ta	mi ˈnat: tʃa
e	**mia**	**vita**	**minaccia,**
and	*my*	*life*	*threatens*

ˈsker tso	e	ˈbe vo
scherzo	**e**	**bevo,**
I joke	*and*	*I drink*

e	de ˈɾi do	ʎin ˈsa ni
e	**derido**	**gl'insani**
and	*I mock*	*the crazy ones*

ke	si	dan	del	fu ˈtu ɾo
che	**si**	**dan**	**del**	**futuro**
who	*themselves*	*devote [to]*	*of the*	*future*

pen ˈsjɛr
pensier.
thought

LE NOZZE DI FIGARO

music: Wolfgang Amadeus Mozart
libretto: Lorenzo da Ponte (after *La Folle Journée, ou Le Mariage de Figaro,* a comedy by Pierre Augustin Caron de Beaumarchais)

Non so più cosa son

non	sɔ	pju	ˈkɔ za	son	ˈkɔ za	ˈfat: tʃo
Non	**so**	**più**	**cosa**	**son,**	**cosa**	**faccio;**
not	*I know*	*more*	*what*	*I am*	*what*	*I do*

or	di	ˈfɔ ko	ˈo ɾa	ˈso no	di	ˈgjat: tʃo
or	**di**	**foco,**	**ora**	**sono**	**di**	**ghiaccio.**
now	*of*	*fire*	*now*	*I am*	*of*	*ice*

ˈoɲ: ɲi	ˈdɔn: na	kan ˈdʒar	di	ko ˈlo ɾe
Ogni	**donna**	**cangiar**	**di**	**colore,**
every	*woman*	*to change*	*of*	*color*

ˈoɲ: ɲi	ˈdɔn: na	mi	fa	pal pi ˈtar
ogni	**donna**	**mi**	**fa**	**palpitar.**
every	*woman*	*me*	*makes*	*to palpitate*

ˈso lo	ˈa i	ˈno mi	da ˈmor	di	di ˈlɛt: to
Solo	**ai**	**nomi**	**d'amor,**	**di**	**diletto,**
only	*at the*	*names*	*of love*	*of*	*pleasure*

mi	si ˈturba	mi	ˈsal te ɾa	il	ˈpɛt: to
mi	**si turba,**	**mi**	**s'altera**	**il**	**petto,**
to me	*becomes upset*	*to me*	*becomes nervous*	*the*	*breast*

e	a	par ˈla ɾe	mi	ˈsfɔr tsa	da ˈmo ɾe	un	de ˈzi o
e	**a**	**parlare**	**mi**	**sforza**	**d'amore**	**un**	**desio,**
and	*to*	*[to] talk*	*me*	*forces*	*of love*	*a*	*desire*

un	de ˈzi o	ˈki o	non	ˈpɔs: so	spje ˈgar
un	**desio**	**ch'io**	**non**	**posso**	**spiegar.**
a	*desire*	*which I*	*not*	*[I] am able*	*to explain*

ˈpar lo	da ˈmor	veʎː ˈʎan do
Parlo	**d'amor**	**vegliando,**
I talk	*of love*	*being awake*

ˈpar lo	da ˈmor	soɲː ˈɲan do
parlo	**d'amor**	**sognando,**
I talk	*of love*	*dreaming*

alː ˈlakː kwa	alː ˈlom bra	ˈa i	ˈmon ti
all'acqua,	**all'ombra,**	**ai**	**monti,**
to the water	*to the shade*	*to the*	*mountains*

ˈa i	ˈfjo ɾi	alː ˈlɛr be	ˈa i	ˈfon ti
ai	**fiori,**	**all'erbe,**	**ai**	**fonti,**
to the	*flowers*	*to the grass*	*to the*	*fountains*

alː ˈlɛ ko	alː ˈla ɾja	ˈa i	ˈvɛn ti
all'eco,	**all'aria,**	**ai**	**venti,**
to the echo	*to the air*	*to the*	*winds*

ke	il	swɔn	de	ˈva ni	atː ˈtʃɛn ti
che	**il**	**suon**	**de'**	**vani**	**accenti**
which	*the*	*sound*	*of [the]*	*in vain*	*words*

ˈpor ta no	ˈvi a	kon	se
portano	**via**	**con**	**se.**
[they] carry	*away*	*with*	*themselves*

e	se	non	ɔ	ki	ˈmɔ da
E	**se**	**non**	**ho**	**chi**	**m'oda,**
and	*if*	*not*	*I have*	*one who*	*to me listens*

ˈpar lo	da ˈmor	kon	me
parlo	**d'amor**	**con**	**me.**
I talk	*of love*	*with*	*myself*

Voi, che sapete

ˈvo i	ke	sa ˈpe te	ke	ˈkɔ za	ɛ	a ˈmor
Voi,	**che**	**sapete**	**che**	**cosa**	**è**	**amor,**
you	*who*	*[you] know*	*what*	*thing*	*is*	*love*

ˈdɔnː ne	ve ˈde te	ˈsi o	lɔ	nel	kɔr
donne,	**vedete,**	**s'io**	**l'ho**	**nel**	**cor.**
ladies	*see*	*if I*	*it [I] have*	*in the*	*heart*

ˈkwelː lo	ˈki o	ˈprɔ vo	vi	ri di ˈrɔ
Quello	**ch'io**	**provo,**	**vi**	**ridirò;**
that	*which I*	*[I] experience*	*to you*	*I will tell again*

ɛ	per	me	ˈnwɔ vo	ka ˈpir	nol	sɔ
è	**per**	**me**	**nuovo,**	**capir**	**nol**	**so.**
it is	*for*	*me*	*new*	*to understand*	*not it*	*I am able*

ˈsɛn to	un	afː ˈfɛtː to	pjen	di	de ˈzir
Sento	**un**	**affetto**	**pien**	**di**	**desir,**
I feel	*an*	*affection*	*full*	*of*	*desire*

ˈko ɾa	ɛ	di ˈlɛtː to	ˈko ɾa	ɛ	mar ˈtir
ch'ora	**è**	**diletto,**	**ch'ora**	**è**	**martir.**
which now	*is*	*pleasure*	*which now*	*is*	*torture*

ˈdʒɛ lo	e	ˈpɔ i	ˈsɛn to	ˈlal ma
Gelo,	**e**	**poi**	**sento**	**l'alma**
I freeze	*and*	*then*	*I feel*	*the soul*

av: vam ˈpar
avvampar,
to burst into flames

e	in	un	mo ˈmen to	ˈtor no	a	dʒe ˈlar
e	**in**	**un**	**momento**	**torno**	**a**	**gelar.**
and	*in*	*a*	*moment*	*I return*	*to*	*[to] freeze*

ri ˈtʃer ko	un	ˈbɛ ne	ˈfwɔ ɾi	di	me
Ricerco	**un**	**bene**	**fuori**	**di**	**me—**
I search for	*a*	*happiness*	*outside*	*of*	*me*

non	sɔ	ki	il	ˈtjɛ ne
non	**so**	**chi**	**il**	**tiene,**
not	*I know*	*who*	*it*	*holds*

non	sɔ	kɔ ˈzɛ
non	**so**	**cos'è.**
not	*I know*	*what it is*

so ˈspi ɾo	e	ˈdʒɛ mo	ˈsɛn tsa	vo ˈler
Sospiro	**e**	**gemo**	**senza**	**voler;**
I sigh	*and*	*I moan*	*without*	*to wish to*

ˈpal pi to	e	ˈtrɛ mo	ˈsɛn tsa	sa ˈper
palpito	**e**	**tremo**	**senza**	**saper.**
I palpitate	*and*	*I tremble*	*without*	*to know why*

non	ˈtrɔ vo	ˈpa tʃe	ˈnɔt: te	ne	di
Non	**trovo**	**pace**	**notte**	**nè**	**dì,**
not	*I find*	*peace*	*night*	*nor*	*day*

ma	pur	mi	ˈpja tʃe	laŋ ˈgwir	ko ˈzi
ma	**pur**	**mi**	**piace**	**languir**	**così,**
but	*yet*	*to me*	*it is pleasing*	*to languish*	*thus*

ORFEO ED EURIDICE

music: Christoph Willibald von Gluck
libretto: Raniero de' Calzabigi (based on Greek mythology)

Che farò senza Euridice?

a i ˈmɛ	ˈdo ve	tra ˈskor si
Ahimè!	**Dove**	**trascorsi?**
alas	*where*	*I passed through*

ˈdo ve	mi	ˈspin se	un	de ˈli ɾjo	da ˈmor
Dove	**mi**	**spinse**	**un**	**delirio**	**d'amor?**
where	*me*	*thrust*	*a*	*delirium*	*of love*

ˈspɔ za	e u ɾi ˈdi tʃe	kon ˈsɔr te
Sposa!	**Euridice!**	**Consorte!**
bride	*Euridice*	*wife*

a	pju	non	ˈvi ve	la	ˈkja mo	in	van
Ah,	**più**	**non**	**vive!**	**La**	**chiamo**	**in**	**van.**
ah	*more*	*not*	*[she] lives*	*her*	*I call*	*in*	*vain*

ˈmi ze ɾo	me	la	ˈpɛr do
Misero	**me,**	**la**	**perdo**
miserable	*me*	*her*	*I lose*

e di ˈnwɔ vo e per ˈsɛm pre
e di nuovo e per sempre!
[and] again and for ever

o ˈled: dʒe o ˈmɔr te
Oh legge! Oh morte!
oh law oh death

o ri ˈkɔr do kru ˈdɛl
Oh ricordo crudel!
oh remembrance cruel

non ɔ sok: ˈkor so
Non ho soccorso,
not I have assistance

non ma ˈvan tsa kon ˈsiʎ: ʎo
non m'avanza consiglio!
not to me advances advice

ˈi o ˈveg: go ˈso lo
Io veggo solo
I [I] see only

o ˈfjɛ ɾa ˈvi sta
(oh fiera vista!)
oh savage sight

il lut: tu ˈo zo a ˈspɛt: to
il luttuoso aspetto
the mournful aspect

del: ˈlɔr: ri do ˈmi o ˈsta to
dell'orrido mio stato.
of the horrible my state

ˈsa tsja ti ˈsɔr te ˈrɛa
Saziati, sorte rea:
satisfy yourself fate wicked

son di spe ˈɾa to
son disperato!
I am desperate

ke fa ˈɾɔ ˈsɛn tsa e u ɾi ˈdi tʃe
Che farò senza Euridice?
what I shall do without Euridice

ˈdo ve an ˈdrɔ ˈsɛn tsa il ˈmi o bɛn
Dove andrò senza il mio ben?
where I shall go without the my beloved

ke fa ˈɾɔ ˈdo ve an ˈdrɔ
Che farò? Dove andrò?
what I shall do where I shall go

ke fa ˈɾɔ ˈsɛn tsa il ˈmi o bɛn
Che farò senza il mio ben?
what I shall do without the my beloved

e u ɾi ˈdi tʃe o ˈdi o ri ˈspon di
Euridice! Oh Dio! Rispondi!
Euridice oh God answer

ˈi o son ˈpu ɾe il ˈtu o fe ˈdel
Io son pure il tuo fedel.
I [I] am still the your faithful one

a non ma ˈvan tsa pju sok: ˈkor so
Ah! non m'avanza più soccorso,
ah not to me advances more assistance

pju spe ˈɾan tsa
più speranza
more hope

ne dal ˈmon do ne dal tʃɛl
nè dal mondo, nè dal ciel!
neither from the world nor from the heaven

IL TROVATORE

music: Giuseppe Verdi
libretto: Salvatore Cammarano, completed by Bardare at Cammarano's death in 1852
(after the play *El Trovador* by Antonio Garcia Gutiérrez)

Stride la vampa!

ˈstri de la ˈvam pa
Stride la vampa!
crackles the blaze

la ˈfol: la in ˈdɔ mi ta
La folla indomita
the crowd indomitable

ˈkor: re a kwel ˈfɔ ko
corre a quel foco
runs to that fire

ˈljɛ ta in sem ˈbjan tsa
lieta in sembianza!
happy in countenance

ˈur li di ˈdʒɔ ja
Urli di gioia
shrieks of joy

in ˈtor no ek: ˈked: dʒa no
intorno eccheggiano;
all around [they] echo

ˈtʃin ta di ˈzgɛr: ri
cinta di sgherri
encircled by ruffians

ˈdɔn: na sa ˈvan tsa
donna s'avanza!
woman approaches

si ˈni stra ˈsplɛn de
Sinistra splende
sinister shines

ˈsu i ˈvol ti or: ˈri bi li
sui volti orribili
on the faces horrible

la ˈtɛ tra ˈfjam: ma
la tetra fiamma
the dreadful flame

ke ˈsal tsa al tʃɛl
che s'alza al ciel!
which rises up to the sky

ˈstri de la ˈvam pa
Stride la vampa!
crackles the blaze

ˈdʒun dʒe la ˈvit: ti ma
Giunge la vittima
arrives the victim

ˈne ɾo ve ˈsti ta
nero vestita,
black dressed in

diʃ: ˈʃin ta e ˈskal tsa
discinta e scalza!
dishevelled and barefoot

ˈgri do fe ˈɾo tʃe
Grido feroce
cry ferocious

di ˈmɔr te ˈle va si
di morte levasi;
of death rises up

ˈlɛ ko il ri ˈpe te
l'eco il ripete
the echo it repeats

di ˈbal tsa in ˈbal tsa
di balza in balza!
from cliff to cliff

ABOUT THE FRENCH IPA TRANSLITERATIONS

by Martha Gerhart

Following is a table of pronunciation for French lyric diction in singing as transliterated in this volume.

THE VOWELS

symbol	nearest equivalent in English	descriptive notes
[ɑ]	as in "father"	the "dark 'a'"
[a]	in English only in dialect; comparable to the Italian "a"	the "bright 'a'"
[e]	no equivalent in English; as in the German "Schnee"	the "closed 'e'": [i] in the [ɛ] position
[ɛ]	as in "bet"	the "open 'e'"
[i]	as in "feet"	
[o]	no equivalent in English as a pure vowel; approximately as in "open"	the "closed 'o'"
[ɔ]	as in "ought"	the "open 'o'"
[u]	as in "blue"	
[y]	no equivalent in English	[i] sustained with the lips rounded to a [u] position
[ø]	no equivalent in English	[e] sustained with the lips rounded almost to [u]
[œ] *	as in "earth" without pronouncing any "r"	[ɛ] with lips in the [ɔ] position
[ɑ̃]	no equivalent in English	the nasal "a": [ɔ] with nasal resonance added
[ɔ̃]	no equivalent in English	the nasal "o": [o] with nasal resonance added
[ɛ̃]	no equivalent in English	the nasal "e": as in English "cat" with nasal resonance added
[œ̃]	no equivalent in English	the nasal "œ": as in English "uh, huh" with nasal resonance added

* Some diction manuals transliterate the neutral, unstressed syllables in French as a "schwa" [ə]. Refer to authoritative published sources concerning such sophistications of French lyric diction.

THE SEMI-CONSONANTS

symbol	nearest equivalent in English	descriptive notes
[ɥ]	no equivalent in English	a [y] in the tongue position of [i] and the lip position of [u]
[j]	as in "ewe," "yes"	a "glide"
[w]	as in "we," "want"	

THE CONSONANTS

[b]	as in "bad"	with a few exceptions
[c]	[k], as in "cart"	with some exceptions
[ç]	as in "sun"	when initial or medial, before *a*, *o*, or *u*
[d]	usually, as in "door"	becomes [t] in liaison
[f]	usually, as in "foot"	becomes [v] in liaison
[g]	usually, as in "gate"	becomes [k] in liaison; see also [ʒ]
[k]	as in "kite"	
[l]	as in "lift"	with some exceptions
[m]	as in "mint"	with a few exceptions
[n]	as in "nose"	with a few exceptions
[ɲ]	as in "onion"	almost always the pronunciation of the "gn" combination
[p]	as in "pass"	except when silent (final) and in a few rare words
[r] *	no equivalent in English	flipped (or occasionally rolled) "r"
[s]	as in "solo"	with exceptions; becomes [z] in liaison
[t]	as in "tooth"	with some exceptions
[v]	as in "voice"	
[x]	[ks] as in "extra," [gz] as in "exist," [z] as in "Oz," or [s] as in "sent"	becomes [z] in liaison
[z]	as in "zone"	with some exceptions
[ʒ]	as in "rouge"	usually, "g" when initial or mediant before *e*, *i*, or *y*; also, "j" in any position
[ʃ]	as in "shoe"	

* The conversational "uvular 'r'" is used in popular French song and cabaret but is not considered appropriate for singing in the classical repertoire.

LIAISON AND ELISION

Liaison is common in French. It is the sounding (linking) of a normally silent final consonant with the vowel (or mute h) beginning the next word. Its use follows certain rules; apart from the rules, the final choice as to whether or not to make a liaison depends on good taste and/or the advice of experts.

Examples of liaison, with their IPA:

les oiseaux	est ici
lɛ‿ zwa zo	ɛ‿ ti si

Elision is the linking of a consonant followed by a final unstressed *e* with the vowel (or mute *h*) beginning the next word.

examples, with their IPA:

elle est	votre âme
ɛ‿ lɛ	vɔ‿ tra mœ

The linking symbol [‿] is given in these transliterations for both **elision** and for (recommended) **liaisons**.

CARMEN

music: Georges Bizet
libretto: Henri Meilhac and Ludovic Halévy (after the novel by Prosper Mérimée)

L'amour est un oiseau rebelle
(Habanera)

la mur	ɛ‿	tœ̃‿	nwa zo	rœ bɛ lœ
L'amour	**est**	**un**	**oiseau**	**rebelle**
the love	*is*	*a*	*bird*	*rebellious*

kœ	nyl	nœ	pø‿	ta pri vwa ze
que	**nul**	**ne**	**peut**	**apprivoiser,**
which	*no one*	*not*	*is able*	*to tame*

e	sɛ	bjɛ̃‿	nɑ̃	vɛ̃
et	**c'est**	**bien**	**en**	**vain**
and	*it is*	*well*	*in*	*vain*

kɔ̃	la pɛ lœ
qu'on	**l'appelle,**
that one	*him calls*

sil	lɥi	kɔ̃ vjɛ̃ dœ	rœ fy ze
s'il	**lui**	**convient de**	**refuser!**
if it	*him*	*suits*	*to refuse*

rjɛ̃	ni	fɛ
Rien	**n'y**	**fait,**
nothing	*not there*	*makes*

mœ na‿	su	pri ɛ rœ
menace	**ou**	**prière—**
threat	*or*	*entreaty*

lœ̃	par lœ	bjɛ̃
l'un	**parle**	**bien,**
the one	*speaks*	*well*

lo trœ	sœ tɛ
l'autre	**se tait;**
the other	*is silent*

e	sɛ	lo trœ
et	**c'est**	**l'autre**
and	*it is*	*the other*

kœ	ʒœ	pre fɛr ə
que	**je**	**préfère—**
whom	*I*	*prefer*

il	na	rjɛ̃	di
il	**n'a**	**rien**	**dit,**
he	*not has*	*anything*	*said*

mɛ‿	zil	mœ	plɛ
mais	**il**	**me**	**plaît.**
but	*he*	*me*	*pleases*

la mur
L'amour!
the love

la mu‿	rɛ‿	tɑ̃ fɑ̃	dœ	bɔ ɛm ə
L'amour	**est**	**enfant**	**de**	**Bohême;**
the love	*is*	*child*	*of*	*Bohemia*

il	na	ʒa mɛ	kɔ ny	dœ	lwa
il	**n'a**	**jamais**	**connu**	**de**	**loi.**
he	*not has*	*ever*	*been acquainted*	*with*	*law*

si	ty	nœ	mɛ mœ	pɑ
Si	**tu**	**ne**	**m'aimes**	**pas,**
if	*you*	*not*	*me love*	*[not]*

ʒœ	tɛ mœ
je	**t'aime;**
I	*you love*

mɛ	si	ʒœ	tɛ mœ
mais	**si**	**je**	**t'aime,**
but	*if*	*I*	*you love*

prɑ̃	gar‿	da	twa
prends	**garde**	**à**	**toi!**
take	*care*	*for*	*yourself*

lwa zo	kœ	ty	krwɑ jɛ	syr prɑ̃ drœ
L'oiseau	**que**	**tu**	**croyais**	**surprendre**
the bird	*which*	*you*	*thought*	*to catch unawares*

ba ti dœ	lɛ‿	le	sɑ̃ vɔ la
battit de	**l'aile**	**et**	**s'envola.**
flapped	*the wing*	*and*	*flew away*

la mu‿	rɛ	lwɛ̃
L'amour	**est**	**loin—**
the love	*is*	*far away*

ty	pø	la tɑ̃ drœ
tu	**peux**	**l'attendre;**
you	*can*	*it await*

ty	nœ	la tɑ̃	ply
tu	**ne**	**l'attends**	**plus,**
you	*not*	*it await*	*anymore*

i‿	lɛ	la
il	**est**	**là!**
it	*is*	*there*

tu‿ to tur dœ	twa
Tout autour de	**toi,**
all around	*you*

vi tœ	il	vjɛ̃	sɑ̃ va
vite,	**il**	**vient,**	**s'en va,**
quickly	*it*	*comes*	*it goes away*

pɥi‿	zil	rœ vjɛ̃
puis	**il**	**revient.**
then	*it*	*comes back again*

ty	krwɑ	lœ	tœ nir
Tu	**crois**	**le**	**tenir,**
you	*think*	*it*	*to have hold of*

il	te vi tə
il	**t'évite;**
it	*you shuns*

ty	krwɑ	le vi te
tu	**crois**	**l'éviter,**
you	*think*	*it to shun*

il	tœ	tjɛ̃
il	**te**	**tient!**
it	*you*	*takes hold of*

la mur
L'amour!
the love

Près des remparts de Séville
(Seguidilla)

prɛ	dɛ	rɑ̃ par	dœ	se vi jə
Près	**des**	**remparts**	**de**	**Séville,**
near	*to the*	*ramparts*	*of*	*Seville*

ʃe	mɔ̃‿	na mi	li lɑs	pa stja
chez	**mon**	**ami**	**Lillas**	**Pastia,**
at the house of	*my*	*friend*	*Lillas*	*Pastia*

ʒi re	dɑ̃ se	la	se gœ di‿
j'irai	**danser**	**la**	**Séguedille**
I will go	*to dance*	*the*	*seguidilla*

je	bwa rœ	dy	man tsa ni ja
et	**boire**	**du**	**manzanilla.**
and	*to drink*	*some*	*manzanilla*

ʒi re	ʃe	mɔ̃‿	na mi	li lɑs	pa stja
J'irai	**chez**	**mon**	**ami**	**Lillas**	**Pastia.**
I will go	*to the house of*	*my*	*friend*	*Lillas*	*Pastia*

wi	mɛ	tu tœ	sœ‿	lɔ̃	sɑ̃ nɥi
Oui,	**mais**	**toute**	**seule**	**on**	**s'ennuie,**
yes	*but*	*all*	*alone*	*one*	*is bored*

e	lɛ	vrɛ	plɛ sir	sɔ̃‿	ta dø
et	**les**	**vrais**	**plaisirs**	**sont**	**à deux;**
and	*the*	*real*	*pleasures*	*are*	*at two [i.e., in twosome]*

dɔ̃k	pur	mœ	tœ nir	kɔ̃ pa ɲi œ
donc,	**pour**	**me**	**tenir**	**compagnie,**
so	*for*	*me*	*to keep*	*company*

ʒɑ̃ mɛ nœ re	mɔ̃‿	na mu rø
j'emmènerai	**mon**	**amoureux!**
I will take with me	*my*	*lover*

mɔ̃‿	na mu rø	i‿	lɛ‿	to	djɑ blœ
Mon	**amoureux!...**	**il**	**est**	**au**	**diable!**
my	*lover*	*he*	*is*	*of the*	*devil*

ʒœ	le	mi‿	za la pɔr‿	ti ɛr
Je	**l'ai**	**mis**	**à la porte**	**hier!**
I	*him have*	*put*	*out the door*	*yesterday*

mɔ̃ po vrœ kœr trɛ kɔ̃ sɔ la blœ
Mon pauvre cœur, très consolable,
my poor heart very consolable

ɛ li brœ kɔ mœ lɛr
est libre comme l'air!
is free as the air

ʒe dɛ ga lɑ̃‿ za la du zɛ nə
J'ai des galants à la douzaine,
I have of lovers by the dozen

mɛ‿ zil nœ sɔ̃ pɑ‿ za mɔ̃ gre
mais ils ne sont pas à mon gré.
but they not are [not] to my taste

vwa si la fɛ̃ dœ la sœ mɛ nœ
Voici la fin de la semaine:
here is the end of the week

ki vø mɛ me ʒœ lɛ mœ re
Qui veut m'aimer? Je l'aimerai!
who wants me to love I him will love

ki vø mɔ̃‿ nɑ‿ mɛ‿ lɛ‿ ta prɑ̃ drœ
Qui veut mon âme? Elle est à prendre!
who wants my soul it is to [to] take

vu‿ za ri ve o bɔ̃ mɔ mɑ̃
Vous arrivez au bon moment!
you arrive at the good moment

ʒœ ne gɛ rœ lœ tɑ̃ da tɑ̃ drœ
Je n'ai guère le temps d'attendre,
I not have hardly the time of to wait

ka‿ ra vɛk mɔ̃ nu vɛ‿ la mɑ̃
car avec mon nouvel amant
for with my new lover

prɛ dɛ rɑ̃ par dœ se vi jə
près des remparts de Séville,
near to the ramparts of Seville

ʃe mɔ̃‿ na mi li lɑs pa stja
chez mon ami Lillas Pastia,
at the house of my friend Lillas Pastia

nu dɑ̃ sœ rɔ̃ la se gœ di‿
nous danserons la Séguedille
we will dance the seguidilla

je bwa rɔ̃ dy man tsa ni ja
et boirons du manzanilla:
and will drink some manzanilla

tra la la
tra la la...
tra la la

En vain, pour éviter

vwa jɔ̃	kœ	je sɛ	a	mɔ̃	tur
Voyons,	**que**	**j'essaie**	**à**	**mon**	**tour.**
let's see	*that*	*I try*	*at*	*my*	*turn*

ka ro	pi kə
Carreau!	**Pique!**
diamonds	*spades*

la	mɔr	je	bjɛ̃	ly
La	**mort!**	**J'ai**	**bien**	**lu—**
the	*death*	*I have*	*well*	*read*

mwa	da bɔr	ɑ̃ sɥi tœ	lɥi
moi	**d'abord,**	**ensuite**	**lui—**
me	*first*	*then*	*him*

pur	tu	lɛ	dø	la	mɔr
pour	**tous**	**les**	**deux,**	**la**	**mort!**
for	*all*	*the*	*two*	*the*	*death*

ɑ̃	vɛ̃	pu‿	re vi te	lɛ	re pɔ̃ sœ‿	za mɛ rœ
En	**vain,**	**pour**	**éviter**	**les**	**réponses**	**amères,**
in	*vain*	*in order*	*to avoid*	*the*	*answers*	*bitter*

ty	mɛ lœ ra
tu	**mêleras!**
you	*will shuffle*

sœ la	nœ	sɛ‿	ra	rjɛ̃
Cela	**ne**	**sert**	**à**	**rien;**
that	*not*	*serves*	*for*	*anything*

lɛ	kar tœ	sɔ̃	sɛ̃ sɛ rœ
les	**cartes**	**sont**	**sincères**
the	*cards*	*are*	*sincere*

e	nœ	mɑ̃ ti rɔ̃	pɑ
et	**ne**	**mentiront**	**pas!**
and	*not*	*they lie*	*[not]*

dɑ̃	lœ	li vrœ	dɑ̃	o
Dans	**le**	**livre**	**d'en**	**haut**
in	*the*	*book*	*from on*	*high*

si	ta	pa‿	ʒɛ‿	tœ rø zə
si	**ta**	**page**	**est**	**heureuse,**
if	*your*	*page*	*is*	*favorable*

mɛ‿	le	ku pœ	sɑ̃	pœr
mêle	**et**	**coupe**	**sans**	**peur:**
shuffle	*and*	*cut*	*without*	*fear*

la	kar tœ	su	tɛ	dwa
la	**carte**	**sous**	**tes**	**doigts**
the	*card*	*under*	*your*	*fingers*

sœ tur nœ ra	ʒwa jø zə
se tournera	**joyeuse,**
will turn up	*joyful*

ta nɔ̃ sɑ̃	lœ	bɔ nœr
t'annonçant	**le**	**bonheur!**
to you announcing	*the*	*good fortune*

mɛ	si	ty	dwa	mu rir
Mais	**si**	**tu**	**dois**	**mourir—**
but	*if*	*you*	*ought*	*to die*

si	lœ	mo	rœ du ta blœ
si	**le**	**mot**	**redoutable**
if	*the*	*word*	*formidable*

ɛ‿	te kri	par	lœ	sɔr
est	**écrit**	**par**	**le**	**sort—**
is	*written*	*by*	*the*	*fate*

rœ kɔ mɑ̃ sœ	vɛ̃	fwa
recommence	**vingt**	**fois,**
[should you] start again	*twenty*	*times*

la	kar‿	tɛ̃ pi twa ja blœ
la	**carte**	**impitoyable**
the	*card*	*merciless*

re pɛ tœ ra	la	mɔr
répétera:	**la**	**mort!**
will repeat	*the*	*death*

wi	si	ty	dwa	mu rir
Oui,	**si**	**tu**	**dois**	**mourir,**
yes	*if*	*you*	*ought*	*to die*

rœ kɔ mɑ̃ sœ	vɛ̃	fwa
recommence	**vingt**	**fois,**
[should you] start again	*twenty*	*times*

la	kar‿	tɛ̃ pi twa ja blœ
la	**carte**	**impitoyable**
the	*card*	*merciless*

re pɛ tœ ra	la	mɔr
répétera:	**la**	**mort**
will repeat	*the*	*death*

ɑ̃ kɔr
Encor!
again

tu ʒur	la	mɔr
Toujours	**la**	**mort!**
always	*the*	*death*

FAUST

music: Charles Gounod
libretto: Jules Barbier and Michel Carré (after the drama by Johann Wolfgang von Goethe)

Faites-lui mes aveux

fɛ tœ lɥi	mɛ‿	za vø
Faites-lui	**mes**	**aveux;**
make to her	*my*	*avowals*

pɔr te	mɛ	vø
portez	**mes**	**vœux!**
bear	*my*	*vows*

flœr‿	ze klo zœ	prɛ	dɛ lœ
Fleurs	**écloses**	**près**	**d'elle,**
flowers	*bloomed*	*near*	*to her*

di tœ lɥi	kɛ‿	lɛ	bɛ lœ
dites-lui	**qu'elle**	**est**	**belle,**
tell her	*that she*	*is*	*beautiful*

kœ	mɔ̃	kœr	nɥi‿	te	ʒur
que	**mon**	**cœur**	**nuit**	**et**	**jour**
that	*my*	*heart*	*night*	*and*	*day*

lɑ̃ gi	da mur
languit	**d'amour!**
languishes	*with love*

re ve le‿	za	sɔ̃‿	nɑ mœ
Révélez	**à**	**son**	**âme**
reveal	*to*	*her*	*soul*

lœ	sœ krɛ	dœ	ma	flɑ mœ
le	**secret**	**de**	**ma**	**flamme,**
the	*secret*	*of*	*my*	*passion*

kil	seg za‿	la vɛk	vu
qu'il	**s'exhale**	**avec**	**vous**
that it	*may exhale*	*with*	*you*

par fœ̃	ply	du
parfums	**plus**	**doux!**
fragrances	*more*	*sweet*

fa ne œ	e lɑs	sœ	sɔr sje
Fanée!	**Hélas!**	**ce**	**sorcier,**
withered	*alas*	*that*	*sorcerer*

kœ	djø	dɑ nə
que	**Dieu**	**damne,**
that	*God*	*damns*

ma	pɔr te	ma lœr
m'a	**porté**	**malheur!**
to me has	*brought*	*bad luck*

ʒœ	nœ	pɥi	sɑ̃	kɛ lœ	sœ fa nœ
Je	**ne**	**puis,**	**sans**	**qu'elle**	**se fane,**
I	*not*	*am able*	*without*	*that it*	*withers*

tu ʃe‿	ry nœ	flœr
toucher	**une**	**fleur!**
to touch	*a*	*flower*

si	ʒœ	trɑ̃ pɛ	mɛ	dwa
Si	**je**	**trempais**	**mes**	**doigts**
if	*I*	*dipped*	*my*	*fingers*

dɑ̃	lo	be ni tœ
dans	**l'eau**	**bénite!**
in	*the water*	*holy*

sɛ	la	kœ	ʃa kœ	swar
C'est	**là**	**que**	**chaque**	**soir**
it is	*there*	*that*	*each*	*evening*

vjɛ̃	pri e	mar gœ ri tœ
vient	**prier**	**Marguerite!**
comes	*to pray*	*Marguerite*

vwa jɔ̃	mɛ̃ tœ nɑ̃
Voyons	**maintenant!**
let us see	*now*

vwa jɔ̃	vi tə
Voyons	**vite!**
let us see	*quickly*

ɛ lœ	sɛ fa nə
Elles	**se fanent?**
they	*wither*

nɔ
Non!
no

sa tɑ̃	ʒœ	ri	dœ	twa
Satan,	**je**	**ris**	**de**	**toi!**
Satan	*I*	*laugh*	*at*	*you*

sɛ‿	tɑ̃	vu	kœ	je	fwa
C'est	**en**	**vous**	**que**	**j'ai**	**foi;**
it is	*in*	*you*	*that*	*I have*	*faith*

par le	pur	mwa
parlez	**pour**	**moi!**
speak	*for*	*me*

kɛ lœ	pɥi sœ	kɔ nɛ trœ
Qu'elle	**puisse**	**connaître**
that she	*may be able*	*to know*

le mwa	kɛ‿	la	fɛ	nɛ trœ
l'émoi	**qu'elle**	**a**	**fait**	**naître,**
the emotion	*that she*	*has*	*made*	*to be born*

e	dɔ̃	mɔ̃	kœr	tru ble
et	**dont**	**mon**	**cœur**	**troublé**
and	*of which*	*my*	*heart*	*troubled*

na	pwɛ̃	par le
n'a	**point**	**parlé!**
not has	*at all*	*spoken*

si	la mur	le fa ru ʃœ
Si	**l'amour**	**l'effarouche,**
if	*the love*	*her startles*

kœ	la	flœr	syr	sa	bu ʃœ
que	**la**	**fleur**	**sur**	**sa**	**bouche**
that	*the*	*flower*	*upon*	*her*	*mouth*

sa‿	ʃo	mwɛ̃	de po ze
sache	**au**	**moins**	**déposer**
may know how	*at*	*least*	*to place*

œ̃	du	bɛ ze
un	**doux**	**baiser!**
a	*sweet*	*kiss*

LES HUGUENOTS

music: Giacomo Meyerbeer
libretto: Eugène Scribe and Emile Deschamps (based on history)

Nobles seigneurs, salut!

nɔ blœ	sɛ ɲœr	sa ly
Nobles	**seigneurs,**	**salut!**
noble	*lords*	*greetings*

y nœ	da mœ	nɔ‿	ble	sa ʒœ
Une	**dame**	**noble**	**et**	**sage,**
a	*lady*	*noble*	*and*	*wise*

dɔ̃	lɛ	rwa	sœ rɛ	ʒa lu
dont	**les**	**rois**	**seraient**	**jaloux,**
of whom	*the*	*kings*	*should be*	*jealous*

ma	ʃar ʒe	dœ	sœ	me sa ʒœ
m'a	**chargé**	**de**	**ce**	**message,**
me has	*entrusted*	*with*	*this*	*message*

ʃœ va lje	pur	lœ̃	dœ	vu
chevaliers,	**pour**	**l'un**	**de**	**vous,**
chevaliers	*for*	*the one*	*of*	*you*

sɑ̃	kɔ̃	la	nɔ mə
sans	**qu'on**	**la**	**nomme,**
without	*that one*	*her*	*names*

ɔ nœ‿	ri si	o	ʒɑ̃ ti jɔ mə
honneur	**ici**	**au**	**gentilhomme**
honor	*here*	*to the*	*gentleman*

kɛ‿	la	ʃwa zi
qu'elle	**a**	**choisi!**
whom she	*has*	*chosen*

vu	pu ve	krwɑ rœ
Vous	**pouvez**	**croire**
you	*can*	*believe*

kœ	nyl	sɛ ɲœr
que	**nul**	**seigneur**
that	*no*	*lord*

ny	tɑ̃ dœ	glwa rœ
n'eut	**tant de**	**gloire**
not had	*so much of*	*glory*

ni	dœ	bɔ nœr	nɔ̃	ʒa mɛ
ni	**de**	**bonheur,**	**non,**	**jamais!**
nor	*of*	*good fortune*	*no*	*never*

nœ	krɛ ɲe	mɑ̃ sɔ̃‿	ʒu	pjɛ ʒœ
Ne	**craignez**	**mensonge**	**ou**	**piège,**
not	*do fear*	*lie*	*or*	*trap*

ʃœ va lje	dɑ̃	mɛ	di skur
chevaliers,	**dans**	**mes**	**discours!**
chevaliers	*in*	*my*	*speech*

ɔr	sa ly	kœ	djø	prɔ tɛ ʒœ
Or	**salut!**	**Que**	**Dieu**	**protège**
now	*goodbye*	*that*	*God*	*may protect*

vo	kɔ̃ ba	vo‿	za mur
vos	**combats,**	**vos**	**amours!**
your	*battles*	*your*	*loves*

ROMÉO ET JULIETTE

music: Charles Gounod
libretto: Jules Barbier and Michel Carré (after the tragedy by William Shakespeare)

Que fais-tu, blanche tourterelle

dœ pɥi‿	zi ɛr	ʒœ	ʃɛr‿	ʃɑ̃	vɛ̃
Depuis	**hier**	**je**	**cherche**	**en**	**vain**
since	*yesterday*	*I*	*search for*	*in*	*vain*

mɔ̃	mɛ trœ
mon	**maître!**
my	*master*

ɛ‿ ti‿	lɑ̃ kɔr	ʃe vu
Est-il	**encore**	**chez vous,**
is he	*still*	*at your house*

mɛ sɛ ɲœr	ka py lɛ
Messeigneurs	**Capulet?**
my lords	*Capulet*

vwa jɔ̃‿	zœ̃	pø	si	vo	di ɲœ	va lɛ
Voyons	**un**	**peu**	**si**	**vos**	**dignes**	**valets**
let's see	*a*	*little*	*if*	*your*	*worthy*	*servants*

a	ma	vwa	sœ	ma tɛ̃	o zœ rɔ̃
à	**ma**	**voix**	**ce**	**matin**	**oseront**
at	*my*	*voice*	*this*	*morning*	*will dare*

rœ pa rɛ trœ
reparaître!
to reappear

kœ	fɛ ty	blɑ̃ ʃœ	tur tœ rɛ lœ
Que	**fais-tu,**	**blanche**	**tourterelle,**
what	*do you*	*white*	*turtledove*

dɑ̃	sœ	ni	dœ	vo tur
dans	**ce**	**nid**	**de**	**vautours?**
in	*that*	*nest*	*of*	*vultures*

kɛl kœ	ʒur	de plwa jɑ̃	tɔ̃‿	nɛ lœ
Quelque	**jour,**	**déployant**	**ton**	**aîle,**
some	*day*	*spreading*	*your*	*wing*

ty	sɥi vra	lɛ‿	za mur
tu	**suivras**	**les**	**amours!**
you	*will follow*	*the*	*loves*

o	vo tur	il	fo	la	ba tɑ jœ
Aux	**vautours**	**il**	**faut**	**la**	**bataille;**
to the	*vultures*	*it*	*is necessary*	*the*	*battle*

pur	fra pe dɛ stɔ‿ ke dœ tɑ jœ
pour	**frapper d'estoc et de taille**
for	*to cut and thrust**

*an idiom; literal translation: to strike with rapier and edge of sword

lœr	bɛk	sɔ̃‿	tɛ gɥi ze
leurs	**becs**	**sont**	**aiguisés!**
their	*beaks*	*are*	*sharpened*

lɛ sœ	la	sɛ‿	zwa zo	dœ	prwɑ œ
Laisse	**là**	**ces**	**oiseaux**	**de**	**proie,**
leave	*there*	*those*	*birds*	*of*	*prey*

tur tœ rɛ lœ	ki	fɛ	ta	ʒwa œ
tourterelle,	**qui**	**fais**	**ta**	**joie**
turtledove	*[you] who*	*make*	*your*	*joy*

dɛ‿	za mu rø	bɛ ze
des	**amoureux**	**baisers!**
from	*amorous*	*kisses*

gar de	bjɛ̃	la	bɛ lœ
Gardez	**bien**	**la**	**belle!**
guard	*well*	*the*	*beautiful one*

ki	vi vra	vɛ ra
Qui	**vivra**	**verra!**
whoever	*will live*	*will see*

vɔ trœ	tur tœ rɛ lœ	vu‿	ze ʃa pœ ra
Votre	**tourterelle**	**vous**	**échappera!**
your	*turtledove*	*you*	*will escape*

œ̃	ra mje	lwɛ̃	dy	vɛr	bɔ ka ʒœ
Un	**ramier,**	**loin**	**du**	**vert**	**bocage,**
a	*wood-pigeon*	*far*	*from the*	*green*	*grove*

par	la mu‿	ra ti re
par	**l'amour**	**attiré,**
by	*the love*	*lured*

a lɑ̃ tur dœ	sœ	ni	so va ʒœ
à l'entour de	**ce**	**nid**	**sauvage**
around	*that*	*nest*	*savage*

a	ʒœ	krwɑ	su pi re
a,	**je**	**crois,**	**soupiré!**
has	*I*	*believe*	*sighed*

lɛ	vo tur	sɔ̃‿	ta	la	ky re ə
Les	**vautours**	**sont**	**à**	**la**	**curée;**
the	*vultures*	*are*	*at*	*the*	*prey*

lœr	ʃɑ̃ sɔ̃	kœ	fɥi	si te re ə
leurs	**chansons**	**que**	**fuit**	**Cythérée**
their	*songs*	*which*	*shuns*	*Cytherea [Aphrodite]*

re zɔ nœ‿	ta	grɑ̃	brɥi
résonnent	**à**	**grand**	**bruit!**
resound	*with*	*great*	*noise*

sœ pɑ̃ dɑ̃	ɑ̃	lœr	du‿	si vrɛ sœ
Cependant,	**en**	**leur**	**douce**	**ivresse,**
meanwhile	*in*	*their*	*sweet*	*intoxication*

no‿	za mɑ̃	kɔ tœ	lœr	tɑ̃ drɛ sœ
nos	**amants**	**content**	**leur**	**tendresse**
our	*lovers*	*satisfy*	*their*	*tenderness*

o‿	za trœ	dœ	la	nɥi
aux	**astres**	**de**	**la**	**nuit!**
at the	*stars*	*of*	*the*	*night*

SAMSON ET DALILA

music: Camille Saint-Saëns
libretto: Ferdinand Lemaire (after the Old Testament, Judges xiv-xvi)

Printemps qui commence

prɛ̃ tɑ̃ ki kɔ mɑ̃ sœ
Printemps qui commence,
spring which begins

pɔr tɑ̃ lɛ spe rɑ̃ sœ
portant l'espérance
bringing the hope

o kœr‿ za mu rø
aux cœurs amoureux,
to the hearts loving

tɔ̃ su flœ ki pɑ sœ
ton souffle qui passe
your breath which passes by

dœ la tɛ‿ re fa sœ
de la terre efface
from the earth erases

lɛ jur ma lœ rø
les jours malheureux.
the days unhappy

tu bry‿ lɑ̃ nɔ‿ trɑ mœ
Tout brûle en notre âme,
everything is on fire in our soul

e ta du sœ flɑ mœ
et ta douce flamme
and your sweet flame

vjɛ̃ se ʃe no plœr
vient sécher nos pleurs;
comes to dry our tears

ty rɑ̃‿ za la tɛ rœ
tu rends à la terre,
you restore to the earth

pa‿ rœ̃ du mi stɛ rœ
par un doux mystère,
through a sweet mystery

lɛ frɥi‿ ze lɛ flœr
les fruits et les fleurs.
the fruits and the flowers

ɑ̃ vɛ̃ ʒœ sɥi bɛ lœ
En vain je suis belle!
in vain I am beautiful

mɔ̃ kœr plɛ̃ da mur
Mon cœur plein d'amour,
my heart full of love

plœ rɑ̃ lɛ̃ fi dɛl
pleurant l'infidèle,
weeping for the infidel

a tɑ̃	sɔ̃	rœ tur
attend	**son**	**retour!**
awaits	*his*	*return*

vi vɑ̃	dɛ spe rɑ̃ sœ
Vivant	**d'espérance,**
living	*with hope*

mɔ̃	kœr	de sɔ le
mon	**cœur**	**désolé**
my	*heart*	*desolate*

gar dœ	su vœ nɑ̃ sœ
garde	**souvenance**
keeps	*memory*

dy	bɔ nœr	pɑ se
du	**bonheur**	**passé!**
of the	*happiness*	*past*

a	la	nɥi	tɔ̃ bɑ̃ tœ
A	**la**	**nuit**	**tombante**
at	*the*	*night*	*falling*

ʒi re	tri‿	sta mɑ̃ tœ
j'irai,	**triste**	**amante,**
I will go	*sad*	*lover*

ma swa‿	ro	tɔ rɑ̃
m'asseoir	**au**	**torrent,**
to seat myself	*by the*	*stream*

la tɑ̃‿	drɑ̃	plœ rɑ̃
l'attendre	**en**	**pleurant!**
him to await	*in*	*weeping*

ʃa sɑ̃	ma	tri stɛ sœ
Chassant	**ma**	**tristesse,**
driving away	*my*	*sadness*

sil	rœ vjɛ̃‿	tœ̃	ʒur
s'il	**revient**	**un**	**jour,**
if he	*comes back*	*one*	*day*

a	lɥi	ma	tɑ̃ drɛ sœ
à	**lui**	**ma**	**tendresse**
to	*him*	*my*	*tenderness*

e	la	du‿	si vrɛ sœ
et	**la**	**douce**	**ivresse**
and	*the*	*sweet*	*intoxication*

kœ̃	bry lɑ̃‿	ta mur
qu'un	**brûlant**	**amour**
which a	*burning*	*love*

gar‿	da	sɔ̃	rœ tur
garde	**à**	**son**	**retour!**
keeps	*for*	*his*	*return*

Amour! viens aider ma faiblesse!

sɑ̃ sɔ̃ rœ ʃɛr ʃɑ̃ ma pre zɑ̃ sœ
Samson, recherchant ma présence,
Samson searching for my presence

sœ swar dwa vœ ni‿ rɑ̃ sɛ ljø
ce soir doit venir en ces lieux.
this evening ought to come to these places

vwa si lœ rœ dœ la vɑ̃ ʒɑ̃ sœ
Voici l'heure de la vengeance
here is the hour of the vengeance

ki dwa sa tis fɛ rœ no djø
qui doit satisfaire nos dieux!
which ought to satisfy our gods

a mur vjɛ̃‿ zɛ de ma fɛ blɛ sœ
Amour! viens aider ma faiblesse!
love come to aid my weakness

vɛr sœ lœ pwa zɔ̃ dɑ̃ sɔ̃ sɛ̃
Verse le poison dans son sein!
pour the poison into his breast

fɛ kœ vɛ̃ ky par mɔ̃‿ na drɛ sœ
Fais que, vaincu par mon adresse,
make that conquered by my skill

sɑ̃ sɔ̃ swa‿ tɑ̃ ʃɛ ne dœ mɛ̃
Samson soit enchaîné demain!
Samson be enchained tomorrow

il vu drɛ‿ tɑ̃ vɛ̃ dœ sɔ̃‿ nɑ mœ
Il voudrait en vain de son âme
he should wish in vain from his soul

pu vwar mœ ʃa se mœ ba nir
pouvoir me chasser, me bannir!
to be able me to drive out me to banish

pu rɛ‿ til e tɛ̃ drœ la flɑ mœ
Pourrait-il éteindre la flamme
could be able he to extinguish the flame

ka li mɑ̃ tœ lœ su vœ nir
qu'alimente le souvenir?
which feeds the memory

i‿ lɛ‿ ta mwa sɛ mɔ̃‿ nɛs klɑ vœ
Il est à moi! C'est mon esclave!
he is mine he is my slave

mɛ frɛ rœ krɛ ɲœ sɔ̃ ku ru
Mes frères craignent son courroux;
my brothers fear his anger

mwa sœl ɑ̃ trœ tus ʒœ lœ bra vœ
moi seule, entre tous, je le brave,
me alone among all I him defy

e le rœ tjɛ̃‿ za mɛ ʒœ nu
et le retiens à mes genoux!
and him detain at my knees

kɔ̃ trœ la mur sa fɔ‿ sɛ vɛ nœ
Contre l'amour, sa force est vaine;
against the love his strength is vain

e lɥi lœ fɔr par mi lɛ fɔr
et lui, le fort parmi les forts —
and he the strong among the strong

lɥi ki dœ̃ pœ plœ rɔ̃ la ʃɛ nœ
lui, qui d'un peuple rompt la chaîne,
he who of a people breaks the chain

sy kɔ̃ bœ ra su mɛ‿ ze fɔr
succombera sous mes efforts!
will succumb beneath my endeavors

Mon cœur s'ouvre à ta voix

mɔ̃ kœr su‿ vra ta vwa
Mon cœur s'ouvre à ta voix
my heart opens up at your voice

kɔ mœ su vrœ lɛ flœr
comme s'ouvrent les fleurs
like open up the flowers

o bɛ ze dœ lɔ rɔ rœ
aux baisers de l'aurore!
at the kisses of the dawn

mɛ o mɔ̃ bjɛ̃ nɛ me
Mais, ô mon bien-aimé,
but o my beloved one

pur mjø se ʃe mɛ plœr
pour mieux sécher mes pleurs,
for better to dry my tears

kœ ta vwa par‿ lɑ̃ kɔ rœ
que ta voix parle encore!
that your voice may speak again

di mwa ka da li la ty rœ vjɛ̃
Dis-moi qu'à Dalila tu reviens
tell me that to Dalila you return

pur ʒa mɛ
pour jamais;
for ever

rœ di‿ za ma tɑ̃ drɛ sœ
redis à ma tendresse
repeat at my tenderness

lɛ sɛr mɑ̃ do trœ fwa
les serments d'autrefois—
the oaths of the past

sɛ sɛr mɑ̃ kœ jɛ mɛ
ces serments que j'aimais!
those oaths which I loved

a re pɔ̃‿ za ma tɑ̃ drɛ sœ
Ah! réponds à ma tendresse!
ah respond to my tenderness

Note: This phrase is usually sung (with a breath taken after "réponds"), as
Ah! réponds, réponds à ma tendresse!
a re pɔ̃ re pɔ̃‿ za ma tɑ̃ drɛ sœ

vɛr sœ mwa li vrɛ sœ
Verse-moi l'ivresse!
pour out to me the intoxication

ɛ̃ si kɔ̃ vwa dɛ ble
Ainsi qu'on voit des blés
as that one sees of the wheat

lɛ‿ ze pi ɔ̃ dy le
les épis onduler
the stalks to undulate

su la bri zœ le ʒɛ rœ
sous la brise légère,
beneath the breeze gentle

ɛ̃ si fre mi mɔ̃ kœr
ainsi frémit mon cœur,
so quivers my heart

prɛ‿ ta sœ kɔ̃ sɔ le
prêt à se consoler
ready to [to] be comforted

a ta vwa ki mɛ ʃɛ rœ
à ta voix qui m'est chère!
at your voice which to me is dear

la flɛ‿ ʃɛ mwɛ̃ ra pi də
La flèche est moins rapide
the arrow ist less quick

a pɔr te lœ tre pɑ
à porter le trépas
to [to] bring the death

kœ nœ lɛ tɔ̃‿ na mɑ̃t
que ne l'est ton amante
than not it is your lover

a vɔ le dɑ̃ tɛ bra
à voler dans tes bras!
to [to] fly into your arms

sɑ̃ sɔ̃ ʒœ tɛ mœ
Samson! je t'aime!
Samson I you [I] love

WERTHER

music: Jules Massenet
libretto: Edouard Blau, Georges Hartmann and Paul Milliet (after the novel *Die Leiden des jungen Werther* by Johann Wolfgang von Goethe)

Va! laisse couler mes larmes

va	lɛ sœ	ku le	mɛ	lar mə
Va!	**laisse**	**couler**	**mes**	**larmes—**
it is alright	*allow*	*to flow*	*my*	*tears*

ɛ lœ	fɔ̃	dy	bjɛ̃	ma	ʃe ri œ
elles	**font**	**du**	**bien,**	**ma**	**chérie!**
they	*do*	*of the*	*good*	*my*	*dear*

lɛ	lar mœ	kɔ̃	nœ	plœ rœ	pɑ
Les	**larmes**	**qu'on**	**ne**	**pleure**	**pas**
the	*tears*	*which one*	*not*	*weeps*	*[not]*

dɑ̃	nɔ‿	trɑ mœ	rœ tɔ̃ bœ	tu tœ
dans	**notre**	**âme**	**retombent**	**toutes,**
into	*our*	*soul*	*fall down*	*all*

e	dœ	lœr	pa si ɑ̃ tœ	gu tœ
et	**de**	**leurs**	**patientes**	**gouttes**
and	*with*	*their*	*enduring*	*drops*

mar tɛ lœ	lœ	kœr	tri‿	te	lɑ
martèlent	**le**	**cœur**	**triste**	**et**	**las!**
hammer	*the*	*heart*	*sad*	*and*	*weary*

sa	re zi stɑ̃ sœ	ɑ̃ fɛ̃	se pɥi zœ
Sa	**résistance**	**enfin**	**s'épuise;**
its	*resistance*	*finally*	*becomes exhausted*

lœ	kœr	sœ krøz	e	sa fɛ bli
le	**cœur**	**se creuse**	**et**	**s'affaiblit:**
the	*heart*	*becomes hollow*	*and*	*grows weak*

i‿	lɛ	trɔ	grɑ̃	rjɛ̃	nœ	lɑ̃ pli
il	**est**	**trop**	**grand,**	**rien**	**ne**	**l'emplit;**
it	*is*	*too*	*big*	*nothing*	*[not]*	*it fills up*

e	trɔ	fra ʒi lœ	tu	lœ	bri zœ
et	**trop**	**fragile,**	**tout**	**le**	**brise!**
and	*too*	*fragile*	*everything*	*it*	*breaks*

ABOUT THE GERMAN IPA TRANSLITERATIONS

by Irene Spiegelman

TRANSLATIONS

As every singer has experienced, word-by-word translations are usually awkward, often not understandable, especially in German where the verb usually is split up with one part in second position of the main clause and the rest at the end of the sentence. Sometimes it is a second verb, sometimes it is a little word that looks like a preposition. Since prepositions never come by themselves, these are usually *separable prefixes to the verb.* In order to look up the meaning of the verb this prefix has to be reunited with the verb in order to find the correct meaning in the dictionary. They cannot be looked up by themselves. Therefore, in the word-by-word translation they are marked with [1]) and do not show any words.

Note: In verbs with separable prefixes, the prefix gets the emphasis. If a separable prefix appears at the end of the sentence, it still needs to be stressed and since many of them start with vowels they even might be glottaled for emphasis.

Also, there are many *reflexive verbs* in German that are not reflexive in English, also the reflexive version of a verb in German often means something very different than the meaning found if the verb is looked up by itself. Reflexive pronouns that are grammatically necessary but do not have a meaning by themselves do not show a translation underneath. They are marked with [2]).

Another difference in the use of English and German is that German is using the Present Perfect Tense of the verb where English prefers the use of the Simple Past of the verb. In cases like that, the translation appears under the conjugated part of the verb and none underneath the past participle of the verb at the end of the sentence. Those cases are marked with [3]).

One last note concerning the translations: English uses possessive pronouns much more often then German does. So der/die/das in German have at appropriate points been translated as my/your/his.

PRONUNCIATION (EXTENDED IPA SYMBOLS)

The IPA symbols that have been used for the German arias are basically those used in Langenscheidt dictionaries. Other publications have refined some symbols, but after working with young singers for a long time, I find that they usually don't remember which is which sign when the ones for long closed vowels (a and ɑ, or ʏ and y) are too close, and especially with the signs for the open and closed u-umlauts they usually cannot tell which they handwrote into their scores. To make sure that a vowel should be closed there is ":" behind the symbol, i.e. [by:p laɪn]

After having been encouraged to sing on a vowel as long as possible, often the consonants are cut too short. The rule is, **"Vowels can be used to make your voice shine, consonants will help your interpretation!"** This is very often totally neglected in favor of long vowels, even when the vowels are supposed to be short. Therefore, double consonants show up here in the IPA line. This suggests that they should at least not be neglected. There are voiced consonants on which it is easy to sing (l, m, n) and often give the text an additional dimension. That is not true for explosive consonants (d, t, k), but they open the vowels right in front of them. So the double consonants in these words serve here as reminders. German does not require to double the consonants the way Italian does, but that Italian technique might help to move more quickly to the consonant, and therefore open the vowel or at least don't stretch it, which sometimes turns it into a word with a different meaning altogether.

One idea that is heard over and over again is: "There is no legato in German." The suggestions that are marked here with ⇨ in the IPA line show that **that is not true.** Always elided can be words ending in a vowel with the next word beginning with a vowel. Words that end with a -t sound can be combined with the next word that starts with a t- or a d-. A word ending in -n can be connected to the following beginning -n. But words ending in consonants can also be elided with the next word starting with a vowel. (example: Dann [dan⇨n] könnt' [kœn⇨n⇨] ich [⇨tɪç] mit [mɪt] Fürsten ['fʏr stən] mich ['mɛs⇨sən]). In this example, the arrow symbol suggests to use the double consonant, but also that the end-t in "könnt'" could be used at the beginning of "ich" which makes the word "ich" much less important (which it usually is in German), and could help to shape the words "Fürsten" and "messen" with more importance.

Within the IPA line, sometimes the "⇨" symbol is only at the end of a word and means that combining this word with the next is absolutely possible if it helps the interpretation of the text or the singer does not want to interrupt the beauty of the musical line. The same fact is true if the "⇨" symbol appears within a word and suggests combining syllables. (Since English syllables are viewed differently than German syllables, the IPA line is broken down into German syllables with suggestions for vocal combinations.) The only consonant that should not be combined with the next word is "r," because there are too many combinations that form new words (example: der Eine, the one and only, should not become [de: raɪ nə], the pure one).

One last remark about pronunciation that seems to have become an issue in the last few years: How does one pronounce the a-umlaut = ä. Some singers have been told in their diction classes that ä is pronounced like a closed e. That may be the case in casual language and can be heard on German television. But when the texts that we are dealing with were written the sound was either a long or short open e sound ['mɛː tçən, ʃpɛːt, 'hɛl tə].

Considering the language, how does one make one's voice shine and still use the text for a sensible interpretation? Look for the words within a phrase that are important to you as the interpreter, as the person who believes what he/she is conveying. In those words use the consonants as extensively as possible. [zzzeː llə] and [llliː bə] are usually more expressive than [zeː lə] and [liː bə] , also glottal the beginning vowels. Use the surrounding words for singing legato and show off the voice.

The IPA line not only shows correct pronunciation but is also giving guidelines for interpretation. For instance, R's may be rolled or flipped, or words may be connected or separated at any time as long as they help you with your feeling for the drama of the text. But you are the person who has to decide! Be discriminating! Know what you want to say! Your language will fit with the music perfectly.

THE “R” IN GERMAN DICTION

When most Germans speak an “r” in front of a vowel, it is a sound produced between the far back of the tongue and the uvula, almost like a gargling sound. The r’s at the end of syllables take on different sounds and often have a vowel-like quality.

In classical singing, the practice is to use “Italian r’s”. Since trilling the r at the tip of the tongue seems to be easy for most singers, many texts are rendered with any overdone r’s, which are remotely possible. As a result, the r’s take over the whole text and diminish the meaning and phrasing of the sentences. By being discriminating in using rolled r’s in an opera text, the phrasing, i.e. interpretation, as well as the chance of understanding the sung text can be improved.

Essentially, there are three categories of words with different suggestions about the use of r’s:

ALWAYS ROLL THE R	**END-R’S IN SHORT ONE-SYLLABLE WORDS**	**END-R’S IN PREFIXES AND SUFFIXES**
a) before vowels: Rose ['roː zə] tragen ['traː gən] sprechen ['ʃprɛː xən] Trug [truːk] führen ['fyː rən] b) after vowels in the main syllable of the word: bergen ['bɛr gən] Herz [hɛrts] Schwert [ʃveːrt] durch [dʊrç] geworben [gə 'vɔr bən] hart [hart]	End-r’s in short one-syllable words that have a closed vowel can be replaced with a short a-vowel, marked in the IPA line with ^{a}. der [deː^{a}] er [eː^{a}] wir [viː^{a}] hier [hiː^{a}] vor [foː^{a}] nur [nuː^{a}] **Note:** **After an a-vowel a replacement of r by ^{a} would not sound. Therefore end-r’s after any a should be rolled.** **war [va:r]** **gar [ga:r]**	Prefixes: ver- er- zer- Here, e and r could be pronounced as a schwa-sound, almost like a short open e combined with a very short ^{a}. If desired, the r could also be flipped with one little flip in order not to overpower the main part of the word which is coming up. In the IPA-line this is marked with ʀ. verbergen [fɛʀ 'bɛr gən] erklären [ɛʀ 'klɛː rən] Suffix: -er These suffixes are most of the time not important for the interpretation of the text. Therefore, the schwa-sound as explained above works in most cases very well. It is marked in the IPA-line with ɚ. e-Suffixes are marked with ə. guter ['guː tɚ] gute ['guː tə] Winter ['vɪn tɚ] Meistersinger ['maɪ stɚ sɪ ŋɚ] (compound noun, both parts end in -er)

DIE FLEDERMAUS

music: Johann Strauss, Jr.
libretto: Carl Haffner and Richard Genée (after the comedy *Le Réveillon* by Henri Meilhac and Ludovic Halévy, which itself was based on the comedy *Das Gefängnis* by Roderich Benedix)

Chacun à son goût

ɪç	ˈlaː də	gɛrn	miː^a	ˈgɛs tə	ˈaɪn
Ich	**lade**	**gern**	**mir**	**Gäste**	**ein;**
I	*invite*	*joyfully*	*to my house*	*guests;*	[1])

man	leːpt	baɪ	miː^a	rɛçt⇨	faɪn
man	**lebt**	**bei**	**mir**	**recht**	**fein.**
one	*celebrates*	*at*	*my house*	*very*	*nicely.*

man	ʊn tɚ ˈhɛl⇨	⇨tsɪç	viː	man	maːk
Man	**unterhält**	**sich**	**wie**	**man**	**mag,**
One	*entertains*	*oneself,*	*however*	*one*	*like,*

ɔft⇨	bɪs⇨	tsʊm	ˈhɛl⇨ lən	taːk
oft	**bis**	**zum**	**hellen**	**Tag.**
often	*till*	*to the*	*bright*	*daylight.*

tsvar	ˈlaŋ vaɪ⇨	⇨lɪç	mɪç	ʃteːts⇨	da ˈbaɪ
Zwar	**langweil'**	**ich**	**mich**	**stets**	**dabei,**
Truthfully,	*am bored*	*I*	[2])	*always*	*during them,*

vas	man⇨	aʊx	traɪpt⇨	ʊnt	ʃprɪçt
was	**man**	**auch**	**treibt**	**und**	**spricht;**
whatever	*people*	*may*	*do*	*and*	*say;*

ɪn ˈdɛs	vas	miː^a	als	vɪrt	ʃteːt	fraɪ
indess',	**was**	**mir**	**als**	**Wirt**	**steht**	**frei,**
but	*what*	*to me*	*as*	*host*	*is allowed*	[1])

dʊlt⇨	ɪç	baɪ	ˈgɛs tən⇨	nɪçt
duld'	**ich**	**bei**	**Gästen**	**nicht.**
endure	*I*	*for (the)*	*guests*	*not.*

ʊn⇨	⇨ˈtseː ə	ɪç	ɛs	ˈañ nyː ˈjiːr⇨	⇨tsɪç
Und	**sehe**	**ich,**	**es**	**ennüyiert**	**sich**
And	*notice*	*I,*	*that*	*is bored*	[2])

ˈjeː mant	hiː^a	baɪ	miː^a
jemand	**hier**	**bei**	**mir,**
someone	*here*	*at*	*my house,*

zoː	pak⇨	⇨kɪç⇨	iːn	gants	ˈʊn ʒeː niːrt
so	**pack'**	**ich**	**ihn**	**ganz**	**ungeniert—**
then	*grab*	*I*	*him*	*quite*	*unabashedly*

vɛrf	iːn	hiː ˈnaʊs⇨	tsuː^a	tyːʀ
werf	**ihn**	**hinaus**	**zur**	**Tür.**
throw	*him*	*out*	*the*	*door.*

ʊnt	ˈfraː gən	ziː	ɪç	bɪt⇨ tə
Und	**fragen**	**Sie,**	**ich**	**bitte,**
And	*if inquire*	*you*	*I*	*ask*

vaː ˈrʊm⇨	ɪç	das	dɛnn	tuː
warum	**ich**	**das**	**denn**	**tu?**
why	*I*	*that*	*after all*	*do?*

sɪst	mal	baɪ	miː^{a}	zoː	zɪt⇨ tə
'sist	**mal**	**bei**	**mir**	**so**	**Sitte:**
It is	*just*	*at*	*my house*	*the*	*custom:*

ʃa kœ̃	a	sɔ̃	guː
chacun	**à**	**son**	**goût!**
Each	*to*	*his own*	*taste!*

vɛnn⇨	ɪç	mɪt	'an dɚn	zɪts	baɪm	vaɪn
Wenn	**ich**	**mit**	**andern**	**sitz**	**beim**	**Wein**
When	*I*	*with*	*others*	*sit*	*having*	*wine*

ʊnt	flaʃ	ʊm	'fla ʃə	leːʀ
und	**Flasch'**	**um**	**Flasche**	**leer',**
and	*bottle*	*after*	*bottle*	*empty,*

mʊss	'jeː dɚ	mɪt	miː^{a}	'dʊr stɪç	zaɪn
muss	**jeder**	**mit**	**mir**	**durstig**	**sein,**
must	*everyone*	*with*	*me*	*thirsty*	*be,*

zɔnst	'veːr də	grɔp⇨	ɪç	zeːʀ
sonst	**werde**	**grob**	**ich**	**sehr.**
or	*become*	*uncivil*	*I*	*very.*

ʊn⇨	⇨tʃɛŋ kə	glaːs⇨	ʊm	glaːs⇨	ɪç	'aɪn
Und	**schenke**	**Glas**	**um**	**Glas**	**ich**	**ein,**
And	*refill*	*glass*	*after*	*glass*	*I*	1)

dʊlt⇨	ɪç	nɪçt	'viː dɚ 'ʃprʊx
duld'	**ich**	**nicht**	**Widerspruch;**
accept	*I*	*no*	*opposition;*

nɪçt	'laɪ dən	kann⇨	ɪçs⇨	vɛn	ziː	ʃraɪn
nicht	**leiden**	**kann**	**ich's,**	**wenn**	**sie**	**schrein:**
not	*bear*	*can*	*I (it)*	*when*	*they*	*shout:*

ɪç	vɪll	nɪçt	haːp	gə 'nuːk
ich	**will**	**nicht,**	**hab'**	**genug!**
I	*want*	*no more,*	*have*	*enough!*

veː^{a}	miː^{a}	baɪm	'trɪŋ kən⇨	nɪçt	paː 'riːʀt
Wer	**mir**	**beim**	**Trinken**	**nicht**	**pariert,**
Whoever	*me*	*in*	*drinking*	*not*	*equals,*

zɪç	'tsiː rət	viː	aɪn	trɔpf
sich	**zieret**	**wie**	**ein**	**Tropf,**
2)	*refuses*	*like*	*a*	*simpleton,*

deːm	'vɛr fə	ɪç	gants	'ʊn ʒeː 'niːʀt
dem	**werfe**	**ich**	**ganz**	**ungeniert**
him	*throw*	*I*	*very*	*unabashedly*

diː	'fla ʃə	an	deːn	kɔpf
die	**Flasche**	**an**	**den**	**Kopf.**
the	*bottle*	*at*	*his*	*head.*

1) Prefixes to the verbs "einladen" (invite), "freistehen" (to be allowed), "einschenken" ((re)fill)

2) Reflexive pronoun to the verbs "sich langweilen" (to be bored), "sich ennüyieren" (to be bored), "sich zieren" (refuse), which are not reflexive in English.

THE INTERNATIONAL PHONETIC ALPHABET FOR ENGLISH

An overview of all the sounds found in American Standard (AS),
British Received (RP), and Mid-Atlantic (MA) Pronunciations.
by Kathryn LaBouff

CONSONANTS:

The following symbols are identical to the letters of our English (Roman) Alphabet:

[b], [d], [f], [g], [h], [k], [l], [m], [n], [p], [s], [t], [v], [w], [z]

The symbols below are NEW symbols added because no corresponding symbols exist in the Roman alphabet:

SYMBOL	KEY WORDS
[ŋ]	sing, think
[θ]	thin, thirst
[ð]	thine, this
[ʍ]	whisper, when
[j]	you, yes
[ʃ]	she, sure
[tʃ]	choose, church
[ʒ]	vision, azure
[dʒ]	George, joy
[ɹ]	red, remember, every (the burred r)
[ʀ]	righteousness, great, realm (rolled r)
[r]	very, far away, forever (flip r used between vowels)

VOWELS:

SYMBOL	KEY WORDS
[ɑ]	father, hot ("o" spellings in AS only)
[ɛ]	wed, many, bury
[ɪ]	hit, been, busy
[i]	me, chief, feat, receive
[ɨ]	pretty, lovely
[t]	cat, marry, ask**, charity
[u]	too, wound, blue, juice
[ju]	view, beautiful, usual, tune
[ɯ]	book, bosom, cushion, full
[o]	obey, desolate, melody (unstressed syllables only)
[ɒ]	on, not, honest, God (RP & MA only)*
[ɔ]	awful, call, daughter, sought (AS)
[ɔ̧]	awful, call, daughter, sought (RP & MA)
[ɝ]	learn, burn, rehearse, journey (AS)
[ɜʳ]	learn, burn, rehearse, journey (RP & MA)
[ɚ]	father, doctor, vulgar, elixir (AS)
[əʳ]	father, doctor, vulgar, elixir (RP & MA)
[ʌ]	hum, blood, trouble, judge (stressed syllables)
[ə]	sofa, heaven, nation, joyous (unstressed syllables)

*The use of rolled and flipped R's and the short open o vowel are used in the British RP British and Mid-Atlantic dialect. They should not be used in American Standard dialect.

**[ɝ and [ɚ] are the r colored vowels characteristic of American Standard Pronunciation, AS.

[ɜʳ] and [əʳ] are the REDUCED r colored vowels found in British RP, and Mid-Atlantic, MA Pronunciations.

DIPHTHONGS:

SYMBOL	KEY WORDS
[aɪ]	night, buy, sky
[eɪ]	day, break, reign
[ɔɪ]	boy, voice, toil
[oʊ]	no, slow, reproach
[ɑʊ]	now, about, doubt
[ɛɚ]	air, care, there (AS)
[ɛəʳ]	air, care, there (RP & MA)
[ɪɚ]	ear, dear, here, tier (AS)
[ɪəʳ]	ear, dear, here, tier (RP & MA)
[ɔɚ]	pour, four, soar, o`er (AS)
[ɔəʳ]	pour, four, soar, o`er (RP & MA)
[ʊɚ]	sure, tour, poor (AS)
[ʊəʳ]	sure, tour, poor (RP & MA)
[ɑɚ]	are, heart, garden (AS)
[ɑəʳ]	are, heart, garden (RP & MA)

TRIPHTHONGS:

SYMBOL	KEY WORDS
[aɪɚ]	fire, choir, admire (AS)
[aɪəʳ]	fire, choir, admire (RP & MA)
[ɑʊɚ]	our, flower, tower (AS)
[ɑʊəʳ]	our, flower, tower (RP & MA)

ADDITIONAL SYMBOLS:

[ˈ] A diacritical mark placed before a syllable that has primary stress.

[ˌ] A diacritical mark placed before a syllable that has secondary stress.

[ɾ] A flapped t or d. It is produced by flapping the tongue against the gum ridge. It is very characteristic of medial t's and d's in coloquial and southern American accents.

[ʔ] A glottalized consonant, usually final or medial t's and d's. It is characteristic of conversational speech patterns in English. Ex: that day- thaʔ day had done- haʔ done

[(ʊ)] An off glide symbol. A weak extra vowel sounded after a primary vowel that is characteristic of certain Southern American accents.

GENERAL NOTES:

The texts in this guide have been transcribed into three primary pronunciations: American Standard, British Received and Mid-Atlantic Pronunciations. American Standard is a neutralized pronuncation of American English that is used for the American stage. British Received Pronunciation is an upper class pronunciation that is the performance standard for British works in the United Kingdom. Mid-Atlantic is a hybrid pronunciation that combines elements of both British and North American pronunciation. Some other variants found in this guide are for colloquial American or American Southern accents.

The standard performance practice for these arias was taken into consideration. The transcriptions were based on the character who sings them, the setting of the opera, and the geographic origin of the works. In general, if the composer and/or the text are North American, then the text is transcribed into American Standard pronunciation or one of the American variants. If the composer and or the text are British, then the text is transcribed into British Received Pronunciation. If the composer is North American but the text is British, then the text is transcribed into Mid-Atlantic. These are guidelines. The pronunciations can be modified to accommodate the production values of a specific operatic production or individual artistic taste.

THE BALLAD OF BABY DOE

music: Douglas Moore
libretto: John Latouche (based on the life of Baby Doe Tabor, 1854–1935)

Augusta! How can you turn away?

In American Standard Pronunciation:

əˈgʌstə haʊ kæn ju tɝn əˈweɪ
Augusta! How can you turn away?

hi wɑz soʊ dɪɚ tu ju ʍɛn ju ˈpɹɑmɪst
He was so dear to you when you promised

ˈɔlˈweɪz tu ˈtʃɛɹɪʃ hɪm
always to cherish him.

ʍɑt kæn hæv ˈhæpənd
What can have happened?

kæn ðɪs bi ju əˈgʌstə
Can this be you, Augusta?

du ju nɑt noʊ ˈhɔɹəs ˈteɪbɚ
Do you not know Horace Tabor?

ɪz hi lɛs ðæn ə ˈstɹeɪndʒɚ
Is he less than a stranger?

goʊ tu hɪm naʊ əˈgʌstə
Go to him now, Augusta.

hoʊld aʊt jɔɚ hænd tu hɪm
Hold out your hand to him.

fɔɚˈgɛt jɔɚ pɹaɪd hi ɪz ɪn ˈtɹʌbəl
Forget your pride; he is in trouble.

naʊ jɔɚ pleɪs ɪz ðɛɚ bɪˈsaɪd hɪm
Now your place is there beside him.

əˈlæs ðə jɪɚz hæv ˈtwɪstəd ju
Alas, the years have twisted you.

ju ɑɚ sɪk ænd oʊld
You are sick and old.

bi ˈkaɪndlɨ ænd bi ˈmɝsɪfʊl
Be kindly and be merciful

bɪˈfɔɚ ɪt ɪz tu leɪt
Before it is too late.

əˈgʌstə ðɪs ɪz jɔɚ ˈfeɪljɚ tu
Augusta! This is your failure too!

ju bɛɚ hɪz neɪm
You bear his name.

ɔlˈðoʊ hi hæz gɹivd ju
Although he has grieved you,

hi stɪl ɪz pɑɚt əv ju
He still is part of you.

ɔl əv ðə ˈmɛmɚɹɨz
All of the memories,

dʒɔɪz ju hæd tʊˈgɛðɚ
joys you had together

kænt bi ˈʌpˈɹutɪd nɑʊ
Can’t be uprooted now,

ðeɪ ɑɚ twaɪnd ɪnˈsaɪd ju
They are twined inside you.

ðə jɪɚz əv ˈbɪtɚnɛs
The years of bitterness,

jɪɚz əv ˈɛmptɨnɛs ænd ˈhɑɚtˈbɹeɪk
Years of emptiness and heartbreak,

ɔl ðiz mʌst pæs fɔɚˈgɑtɪn nɑʊ
All these must pass forgotten now,

nɑʊ ðæt hi nidz ju əˈgʌstə
Now that he needs you, Augusta.

ˈteɪbɚ maɪ ˈhʌzbənd
Tabor, my husband!

ˈteɪbɚ maɪ dɪɚ wʌn
Tabor, my dear one!

ʍaɪ dɪd ju ˈɛvɚ liv mi
Why did you ever leave me?

nɑʊ æt læst
Now at last,

nɑʊ ðæt ˈteɪbɚ nidz əˈgʌstə
Now that Tabor needs Augusta,

aɪ ʃʊd goʊ bʌt aɪ æm əˈfɹeɪd
I should go but I am afraid.

ˈteɪbɚ wʌns lʌvd mi
Tabor once loved me.

wʌns əˈgɛn aɪ hɪɚ hɪm kɔl
Once again I hear him call,

ˈkɔlɪŋ ɑn əˈgʌstə
Calling on Augusta.

bʌt aɪ ˈkæˈnɑt goʊ
But I cannot go.

THE CONSUL

music and libretto: Gian Carlo Menotti

Lullaby

In American Standard Pronunciation:

aɪ ʃæl faɪnd fɔɚ ju ʃɛlz ænd stɑɚz
I shall find for you shells and stars.

aɪ ʃæl swɪm fɔɚ ju ɹɪvɚ ænd si
I shall swim for you river and sea.

slip maɪ lʌv slip fɔɚ mi
Sleep, my love, sleep for me.

maɪ slip ɪz oʊld
My sleep is old.

aɪ ʃæl fid fɔɚ ju læm ænʔ dʌv
I shall feed for you lamb and dove.

aɪ ʃæl baɪ fɔɚ ju ˈʃʊgɚ ænd bɹɛd
I shall buy for you sugar and bread.

slip maɪ lʌv slip fɔɚ mi
Sleep, my love, sleep for me.

maɪ slip ɪz dɛd
My sleep is dead.

ɹeɪn wɪl fɔl bʌt ˈbeɪbɨ woʊnt noʊ
Rain will fall but Baby won't know,

hi læfs əˈloʊn ɪn ˈɔɚtʃɚdz əv goʊld
He laughs alone in orchards of gold.

tɪɚz wɪl fɔl bʌt ˈbeɪbɨ woʊnt noʊ
Tears will fall but Baby won't know.

hɪz læftɚ ɪz blaɪnd
His laughter is blind.

slip maɪ lʌv fɔɚ slip ɪz kaɪnd
Sleep, my love, for sleep is kind.

slip ɪz kaɪnd ʍɛn slip ɪz jʌŋ
Sleep is kind when sleep is young.

slip fɔɚ mi
Sleep for me.

aɪ ʃæl bɪld fɔɚ ju pleɪnz ænd boʊts
I shall build for you planes and boats.

aɪ ʃæl kætʃ fɔɚ ju ˈkɹɪkət ænd bi
I shall catch for you cricket and bee.

lɛt ði oʊld wʌnz wɑtʃ jɔɚ slip
Let the old ones watch your sleep.

ˈoʊnlɨ dɛθ wɪl wɑtʃ ði oʊld
Only death will watch the old.

slip
Sleep.

DIDO AND AENEAS

music: Henry Purcell
libretto: Nahum Tate (after Virgil's *Aeneid, iv*)

When I am laid in earth

In Historic British Received Pronunciation:

ðaɪ   hænd   bɛˈlɪndə
Thy   hand,   Belinda;

ˈdɑɚknɛs   ʃeɪdz   mi
darkness   shades   me,

ɒn   ðaɪ   ˈbʊzəm   lɛt   mi   ʀ/ɹɛst
on   thy   bosom   let   me   rest.

mɔ   r‿aɪ   wʊd   bʌt   dɛθ   ɪnˈveɪdz   mi
More   I   would,   but   Death   invades   me;

ðɛθ   ɪz   nɑʊ   ə   ˈwɛlkəm   gɛst
Death   is   now   a   welcome   guest.

ʍɛn   aɪ   æm   leɪd   ɪn   ɜ^{r}θ
When   I   am   laid   in   earth,

meɪ   maɪ   ʀ/ɹɔŋz   kʀ/ɹiˈeɪt
may   my   wrongs   create

noʊ   tʀ/ɹʌbəl   ɪn   ðaɪ   bʀ/ɹɛst
No   trouble   in   thy   breast.

r/ɹɪˈmɛmbə^{r} mi
Remember   me,

bʌt   ɑ   fɔə^{r}ˈgɛt   maɪ   feɪt
but   ah!   forget   my   fate.

In British Received Pronunciation, all grammatically stressed words that begin with an initial "r" either in a single consonant or in a consonant cluster or group can be either rolled or burred at the artistic discretion of the singer.

THE MOTHER OF US ALL

music: Virgil Thomson
libretto: Gertrude Stein (scenario by Maurice Grosser)

We cannot retrace our steps

In American Standard Pronunciation:

wi ˈkæˈnɑt ˈɹiˈtɹeɪs ɑʊɚ stɛps
We cannot retrace our steps,

ˈɡoʊɪŋ ˈfɔɚwɚd meɪ bi ðə seɪm æz ˈɡoʊɪŋ ˈbækwɚdz
going forward may be the same as going backwards.

wi ˈkæˈnɑt ˈɹiˈtɹeɪs ɑʊɚ stɛps
We cannot retrace our steps.

ɔl maɪ lɔŋ laɪf
All my long life,

ɔl maɪ laɪf
all my life,

wi du nɑt ˈɹiˈtɹeɪs ɑʊɚ stɛps
we do not retrace our steps,

ɔl maɪ lɔŋ laɪf bʌt
all my long life, but.

bʌt wi du nɑt ˈɹiˈtɹeɪs ɑʊɚ stɛps
But we do not retrace our steps,

ɔl maɪ lɔŋ laɪf ænd hɪɚ
all my long life, and here,

hɪɚ wi ɑɚ hɪɚ
here we are here,

ɪn ˈmɑɚbəl ænd goʊld
in marble and gold,

dɪd aɪ seɪ goʊld
did I say gold,

jɛs aɪ sɛd goʊld
yes I said gold,

ɪn ˈmɑɚbəl ænd goʊld ænd ʍɛɚ
in marble and gold and where

ʍɛɚ ɪz ʍɛɚ
Where is where.

ɪn maɪ lɔŋ laɪf əv ɛfɚt ænd stɹaɪf
In my long life of effort and strife,

dɪɚ laɪf laɪf ɪz stɹaɪf
dear life, life is strife,

ɪn maɪ lɔŋ laɪf ɪt wɪl nɑt kʌm ænd goʊ
in my long life, it will not come and go,

aɪ tɛl ju soʊ
I tell you so,

ɪt wɪl steɪ ɪt wɪl peɪ bʌt
it will stay it will pay but

bʌt du wi wɑnt ʍɑt wi hæv gɑt
But do we want what we have got,

hæz ɪt nɑt gɔn ʍɑt meɪd ɪt lɪv
has it not gone, what made it live,

hæz ɪt nɑt gɔn bɪˈkɔz nɑt ɪt ɪz hæd
has it not gone because not it is had,

ɪn maɪ lɔŋ laɪf
in my long life

laɪf ɪz stɹaɪf aɪ wɑz ə ˈmɑɚtɚ ɔl maɪ laɪf
Life is strife, I was a martyr all my life

nɑt tu ʍɑt aɪ wʌn bʌt tu ʍɑt wɑz dʌn
not to what I won but to what was done.

du ju noʊ bɪˈkɔz aɪ tɛl ju soʊ
Do you know because I tell you so,

ɔɚ du ju noʊ du ju noʊ
or do you know, do you know.

maɪ lɔŋ laɪf
My long life.

THE SAINT OF BLEECKER STREET
music and libretto: Gian Carlo Menotti

Ah, Michele, don't you know
In American Standard Pronunciation:

wɛl ðɛn wɪl ju teɪk mi ɪn wɪð ju
Well, then, will you take me in with you?

ˈænsɚ mi
Answer me.

ɑ miˈkele doʊnt ju noʊ
Ah, Michele, don't you know

ðæt lʌv kæn tɝn tu heɪt æt ðə saʊnd əv wʌn wɝd
that love can turn to hate at the sound of one word,

ɪf ðə wɝd ɪz sɛd tu leɪt
if the word is said too late?

lʌv kæn ˈnɛvɚ hil ɪts wundz
Love can never heal its wounds

ənˈlɛs ðə kɹaɪ ɪz ˈænsɚd
unless the cry is answered,

ənˈlɛs ðə skɑɚ ɪz sin
unless the scar is seen.

ɔl ðə tɪɚz wʌn wips əˈloʊn
All the tears one weeps alone

du nɑt ˈʌnˈlɑk ðə ˈpaʊndɪŋ geɪts əv ðə hɑɚt
do not unlock the pounding gates of the heart.

laɪk stɑɚz ðeɪ fɔl
Like stars they fall

ɪn dɛθlɨ ˈstɪlnəs
in deathly stillness

bʌt liv ə ˈpɔɪzɪnd tɹeɪl
but leave a poisoned trail.

ˈoʊnlɨ hi huz tɪɚz ɑɚ ˈmɪɹɚd
Only he, whose tears are mirrored,

kæn bɛɚ ðə ˈsikɹɪt peɪn əv ˈlɪvɪŋ
can bear the secret pain of living.

ðoʊz əv ʌs hu faɪnd ɑʊɚ lʌv ɑn ɝθ
Those of us, who find our love on earth,

mʌst ˈsɛləˈbɹeɪt ɑʊɚ ˈflitɪŋ ˈtɹaɪəmf
must celebrate our fleeting triumph.

hu ˈwɛlkəmz lʌv ɪn ˈsaɪləns
Who welcomes love in silence

ɔɚ haɪdz ɪt laɪk ə kɹaɪm
or hides it like a crime,

ʃæl sun ɹʌn tu ðə ˈweɪstˈlændz
shall soon run to the wastelands

tu ɪsˈkeɪp ɪts ˈblaɪndɪŋ ˈvɛndʒəns
to escape its blinding vengeance.

ɑ miˈkele doʊnt fɔɚˈgɛt ðæt lʌv
Ah, Michele, don't forget that love

ɪz ə ˈpɪtɨlɛs ˈhʌntɚ ʍɛn æˈlaɪd wɪð dɛθ
is a pitiless hunter when allied with death.

VANESSA

music: Samuel Barber
libretto: Gian Carlo Menotti

Must the winter come so soon?

In American Standard Pronunciation:

mʌst ðə ˈwɪntɚ kʌm soʊ sun
Must the winter come so soon?

naɪt ˈæftɚ naɪt
Night after night

aɪ hɪɚ ðə ˈhʌngɹi dɪɚ
I hear the hungry deer

ˈwɑndɚ ˈwipɪŋ ɪn ðə wʊdz
wander weeping in the woods,

ænd fɹʌm hɪz haʊs əv ˈbɹɪtəl bɑɚk
and from his house of brittle bark

huts ðə ˈfɹoʊzən aʊl
hoots the frozen owl.

mʌst ðə ˈwɪntɚ kʌm soʊ sun
Must the winter come so soon?

hɪɚ ɪn ðɪs ˈfɔɹɛst
Here in this forest

ˈnaɪðɚ dɔn nɔɚ ˈsʌnˈsɛt
neither dawn nor sunset

mɑɚks də ˈpæsɪŋ əv ðə deɪz
marks the passing of the days.

ɪt ɪz ə lɔŋ ˈwɪntɚ hɪɚ
It is a long winter here.

mʌst ðə ˈwɪntɚ kʌm soʊ sun
Must the winter come so soon?